Wisdom

LESSONS
FOR TODAY

Timeless Words of Inspiration and Instruction

Alda St. James

WISDOM LESSONS FOR TODAY

Timeless Words of Inspiration and Instruction

Alda St. James

ENDORSEMENTS

"Moses said, "Would that all were prophets!" (Numbers 11: 29). Alda St. James has taken this exhortation seriously and shares with her readers the fruits of her reflections on her faith in Jesus Christ and how it is best lived out in daily life. May her prophetic words inspire others to be prophets of the Lord as well!

Most Reverend Clarence (Larry) Silva

Bishop of Honolulu

Experiential and inspirational wisdom is what I read in "Wisdom Lessons for Today" by Alda St. James. A timely and a 'must-read' offer for every person regardless of age, gender or religious affiliation. Desiring wisdom is a step forward to starting to live (Proverb 2:4).

Rev. Fr. Dr. Byaruhanga Kakaaga Emmanuel

Rector – St. Mary's Seminary, Fort Portal – Uganda (EA)

I

Clear, straight to the point. The mind of the reader is immediately drawn into deep reflective thought, and even moments of ecstasy.

Most Reverend Monsignor Andrew Chunda,

Malawi, Africa

Alda's personal reflections provide readers with a thoughtful and faithful snapshot of God's unending grace and wisdom. Her engaging word choice creates a relatable body of work that can meet people wherever they are at the intersection of spirituality and reason.

Lori Stanley

Executive Director -Loyola Institute for Spirituality, Orange,

CA

Copyright

WISDOM LESSONS FOR TODAY

Timeless Words of Inspiration and Instruction

ISBN: 978-1-7367401-2-5 (kindle)

ISBN: 978-1-7367401-3-2 (Print Book)

First Edition – September 2021

Published by: Prisma Press

Cover design by Alda St. James (http://aldastjames.com/)

Book formatting, publishing & layout by: Exponential Digital Trainers (https://exponentialdigitaltrainers.com/)

DEDICATION

In memory of my father, Savino Longo,

a lover of beauty and a seeker of truth

OTHER BOOKS BY ALDA ST. JAMES

1. Listen To Love: Reflective Poems For All Seasons

2. Birthstone Coloring Book: Birthstone Legends and Other Gem Folklore

A NOTE TO NON-CHRISTIANS

As I began the adventure of writing this book, I had a special concern...

I wanted you, as a non-Christian reader, perhaps as an agnostic or atheist, to gleam some insight from these openly "religious" pages. In my research, I have relied heavily upon biblical texts as well as other spiritual and philosophical writings. Yet, I do not apologize for this because these sources contain perennial wisdom, and they so accurately predict what is happening in our world today. Since I have chosen these texts as references, I am sure some of you will feel alienated, and it will likely deter you from reading this book. If that is the case, I hope you are brave enough to reconsider. Perhaps you are willing to suspend your personal judgement for a brief time, to temporarily consider a cosmology other than your own, to look beyond a mechanistic world view, to step outside your comfort zone.

There is one, crucial reason for doing so. It is that we are ALL called to be children of the Most High. We are all called to Wisdom, Light, and Understanding. If this sounds rather flaky or pious, I invite you - no, I dare you - to pick up this short book and read it. What you will find inside are things you have never heard of before, things that cannot be explained by the most esteemed men and women of our scientific and technological age. Such things underscore the same basic, stubborn truths. Despite denial by the worldly wise, these truths have persisted since time immemorial. Although they are not new, they have been largely forgotten, and it is high time to take a fresh look at them.

The second point I want to make is this: In our present day, there is a kind of convergence happening around the concept of truth. Looking only with materialistic eyes, you may say the opposite is true, that we are becoming more and more fragmented and polarized as a people and as a world. Case in point: there is a huge gap between science and religion, and this gap seems to be getting wider every day. But despite trends to the contrary, I perceive a silent, unseen convergence taking place under the radar. The resulting unification will nullify the friction of opposing sides that is ubiquitous today. Diverse viewpoints will be brought into focus, and they will co-exist in uncanny, innovative ways. Watch for it; it is coming soon!

TABLE OF CONTENTS

PROLOGUE

"At that time, Jesus continued, "I praise you,
Father, Lord of Heaven and earth, that you have
hidden these things from clever and learned people
and have revealed them to little children."

(Matthew 11: 25)

I must apologize. I have written several books without proper credentials. I have published a book of poetry, and now this book of essays. Beyond that, I have not published anything of intellectual consequence, nor did I receive a graduate degree in Theology. Thus, I am probably opening myself up to criticism. Nevertheless, I make no claims whatsoever to justify what I have written. And I suspect some of the essays contained in this book may be controversial or disturbing. But if I were asked to explain by what authority I do this, I have no answer other than this: I listen to the Lord and I am instructed by Him.

It was Fr. Walter Ciszek's classic book written back in

1

1973, "He Leadeth Me," which alerted me to the possibility of negative reviews or worse. Just by recounting and reflecting upon his own experience, Fr. Ciszek encountered criticism. His book didn't sit well with some people who were quick to judge his faith as "childish and naïve." I may receive the same criticism. Yet didn't Jesus say, "Unless you change and become like little children, you will never enter the Kingdom of Heaven" (Matthew 18: 3)?

Know that this book was written with that child-like sense of awe and wonder, as if gazing upon the Divine Reality. As such, I sincerely hope it has some value to those who take the time to read it.

Alda St. James, Author

INTRODUCTION

WISDOM LESSONS FOR TODAY: *Timeless Words of Inspiration and Instruction*, can be read in two ways. You can read the essays in the order they appear, and there is some justification in the particular way I have listed them in the Table of Contents. Yet, it is equally effective to read each one as a stand-alone commentary. Originally, they were composed as simple reflections on various universal topics. As I wrote, these topics expanded from just a few to seventeen, and their scope broadened to encompass common concerns which concerns which everyone can relate to.

In each essay, ancient maxims from various spiritual sources are cited as references. I pair these with some of the ordinary happenings we all encounter daily, as well as with current events. Therefore, they are relevant; the essays reveal how ancient, as well as modern spiritual writings apply perfectly to both our immediate, personal problems, and to the present age in which we live. When current and potential future developments are discussed, I show how precise biblical passages relate to these events. Indeed, there is a universality in ancient texts which is undeniable. This may be why the Bible is the most popular book, in terms of sales, ever written. Because of the inherent fragility and vulnerability of the human condition, the perennial wisdom the Bible imparts continues to speak to us today. What is amazing is that the wise counsel it offers for our most pressing concerns is as fresh, timeless, and appropriate as it was when it was first compiled so long ago.

*Editor's Note: *In some of the essays the author uses italics and capital letters in order to emphasize a point.*

LESSON ONE

THE EVOLUTION OF

FREEWILL

THE EVOLUTION OF

FREEWILL

"Live as free men yet without using your freedom as a cloak for evil but live as servants of God."

(1 Peter 2: 16)

Three Stages of the Will

Most people believe we have freewill, that is, the freedom to choose right from wrong. When we teach our children, we teach them that they can make good or bad choices. Likewise, Christians believe that freewill is our God-given birthright. In the Old Testament, Deuteronomy 30: 19 says that from the beginning God set before us, "Life and death, blessings and cursings," and we must choose between them. (See Lesson 5 in this series, "Choose Life"). In the New Testament, Jesus continues this teaching and exemplifies it by His own life. He reminds us of our freedom to choose, and in a singular act of love, Jesus invites us to follow Him. If we accept His invitation, we receive the opportunity to respond to God's grace in an entirely new way. This is the "New Covenant" that Jesus established; it reveals the gift of eternal life which, by His supreme sacrifice, Jesus freely offers to everyone. But we always have the freedom to reject this grace, the Son whom God sent, our salvation, and eternal life. Therefore, the use of our will is of critical importance. Anyone who believes in life after death can agree; the thoughts and actions we choose today will ultimately determine the destiny of our souls in a very real way.

I know there are some Christians, perhaps many, who argue that Faith alone is enough to be saved. I will put aside the Faith vs. Works controversy for now, since I wish to concentrate on the role freewill plays in drawing us closer to God here and now, as we live our lives on earth each day.

Whether you know it or not, all of us are on a spiritual journey. It consists of attuning ourselves more and more to a higher Power or Consciousness, or to put it another way, to become aware of and more compliant with the Divine Will. The German theologian Johannes Baptist Metz, acknowledges this in his book, "Poverty of Spirit." He says, "When the mask falls, and the core of our being is revealed, it soon becomes obvious that we are religious by nature." As we gain this insight, I propose that an evolution takes place within us, a natural progression of our freewill. I believe this happens in three distinct stages or steps: They are "The Will to Do Good," then "Purity of Conscience," and finally "Complete Trust."

The Will to Do Good

Certainly, the world is full of sincere people who habitually decide to do charitable work, and many do it without religious ties; some do not believe in God at all. What can we say about all the good works these people do? Surely God acknowledges them. Jesus answers this question directly when he says, "If you do good to those who do good to you, what credit is that to you? Even sinners do as much!" (Luke 6: 33). And Jesus warns, "Do not do good things so that people will see you do them. If you do, you will get no reward from your Father in Heaven" (Matthew 6: 1). Clearly, Jesus wants more from us then assisting those who reciprocate or being satisfied with others' approval. Reflecting on Jesus' remarks, we may find them hard to swallow, perhaps even a bit harsh. Is it possible that our outward displays of "goodness" are not the whole story?

8

Well, let's see...

We know that when a person decides to do a good deed, he may have any number of "good" reasons. Perhaps he wants to impress his friends and family as someone who is charitable. Or he may like a particular person and sincerely want to help him/her succeed. Maybe he feels guilty about not doing more for a worthy social cause, and so he responds by giving. When we look deeper at these motives, one thing stands out; this altruism is not as much about giving as we first thought. It is more about the giver's social status, how generous he appears to others, or how he chooses to define himself. Looking at it from this perspective, it seems as though any act of giving may easily be tainted by our own personal interests, our individual needs, preferences, and desires. If giving has little or nothing to do with God, and it is more about one's self-image, then we can see where Jesus' words ring true. Remember in Matthew 7: 21, Jesus tells us, "Not everyone who says to Me, 'Lord, Lord,' shall enter the Kingdom of Heaven, but he who does the Will of My Father in Heaven. "This means there has to be more to our efforts to do good than what is merely obvious or superficial.

Because this is true, introspection is always beneficial. In

Catholic parlance, it's called, "Examination of Conscience." As we practice this exercise in introspection, we begin to unveil any hidden agendas, revealing what our true motivations are. Of course, although not perfect, most of us like to think of ourselves as pretty good people, which is far better than being thought of as uncharitable or selfish. But I wonder, is "being good" good enough? Although we may have developed "The Will to Do Good," our rudimentary charity or goodness represents only the beginning of a life-long quest. God wills "that no soul should perish but...has provided a way of escape" (2 Peter 3: 9). Likewise, it can be argued that a sincere desire to do good is the first step along that way of escape which St. Paul describes in Scripture (1 Corinthians 10: 13).

From here, faith becomes our core value. As Christians, we must decide that our faith always precedes any plan of action we undertake. Only after acknowledging this can, we have confidence that a decision in any matter, our "will act," carries real value. So always start by becoming centered in Jesus. In doing so, we can begin to stop focusing entirely on what we want and start seeking what God wants for us. Thus, our "good" desires are elevated to a higher level. This is why St. Paul tells us to "transform our mind, that by testing you may discern what is the Will of God, what is good, acceptable, and perfect" (Romans 12: 2). Transforming our mind means changing it from simply doing good, positive actions, to pursuing spiritual ones. This leads to the next step, "Purity of Conscience."

Purity of Conscience

Here we discover an even deeper level of our personal intentions and motivations. As we enter this stage, we can look at ourselves without bias. If we begin by asking, "How sincere is my commitment to do good?" the answer may be surprising. This is because, even though we are trying to live up to our highest ideal, the successes we enjoy often turn out to be self-serving anyway, especially if we receive praise or reward for our efforts.

This is an example of what I mean: Let's say you just got promoted. Or you landed a particular, high-paying job which makes excellent use of your skill set. Your desire to have this job may be because you excel at this type of work, the pay and benefits are excellent, the job is close to home, or the position comes with many perks and accolades.

Furthermore, you are delighted that it increases your status and prestige in the community. Although these are all good, solid reasons for wanting the job, self-interest may still be your primary motive. At the end of the day, your desire for a particular job or position may have little to do with your relationship with God or a desire to serve others.

But do not be disheartened. Although our basically "good" deeds can get stuck at the practical level, we can purify them. This is done by simply and consciously deciding that whatever we do, we will do it for God. If you are not particularly religious, you can decide to do your work for the sake of spreading goodness and righteousness in the world. These qualities are, after all, essential aspects of the Divine Nature. Undertaking a regime such as making a daily offering gives those who do it, a spiritual focus and direction; it is a simple gesture which purifies our intentions and allows God, who is Goodness itself, to act in and through us. And as I just said, anyone can make a humble offering by whatever method seems appropriate to them. The important thing is that it is done with purpose and meaning. This is what creates "Purity of Conscience" in us as we go about our daily business. Then, even the most menial task becomes elevated and perfected, and it has great spiritual value no matter what type of work it is. This sentiment is echoed in the Gospels. In Colossians 3: 23, we read, "Whatever your task may be, work at it with your whole being. Do it for the Lord, not for men." Only an act of will make this life-affirming choice: Ask yourself, "Am I doing this or that to advance Goodness in the world or am I doing it just for myself?" This brings us to the third stage, which is "Complete Trust."

Complete Trust

St. James explains, "You believe there is one God. Good! Even the demons believe that - and they shudder" (James 2:19). Obviously, more is expected of us than a simple belief in God. So here's the thing: At this juncture you are asked to extend the faith you already have as far as you can, all the while avoiding evil. Here is where you reach a critical crossroads; a place where you can freely choose to surrender your whole will to the Lord. Why do this? Because you have gained trust, and that's why you can put yourself in the hands of the One who wishes to guide, console, strengthen, and protect you. For sure, to give yourself away requires "Complete Trust." This is especially true if you are uncertain or anxious about what the future holds. There is a little prayer that can act as an excellent remedy for this problem. It is taken from the Society of St. Paul prayer book: "Jesus Master, you are the Way...guide me. You are the Truth...enlighten me. You are the Life... strengthen me" (also see John 14: 6). If you sincerely request help, help is on the way!

But there is a caveat: Sometimes the results of our best efforts seem to be confusing, disappointing, or painful. Yet with every new setback, we are challenged to stand firm, knowing that God is aware of what He is doing even if we are not. Only when the first two stages of freewill - "The Will to Do Good" and "Purity of Conscience" - have been mastered, can we set in motion the last piece of the puzzle which is "Complete Trust" no matter what the circumstance. As I've said, harmful things still can happen, and we do not always understand why some situations turn out badly. Therefore, the third step in "The Evolution of Freewill" is surely the most difficult to achieve, since it requires unflinching patience and sometimes long-suffering. As always, we must be willing to leave the results, all results, to Divine Providence. In 2006, Jesuit priest Fr. James Martin wrote an inspirational book, "My Life with the Saints." In it, the author expresses his understanding of complete trust: "When I'm fighting for something I believe is just, I remember (saint) Joan of Arc; the lifelong fighter reminds me of the need to trust in God, not in results."

The Saints

It is easy to see how the lives of the saints provide the best example for us. This is because the ideal which the saints embody is to do the Will of God perfectly and forsake all else. St. Francis of Assisi said the greatest gift we can receive *from* God is "to know how to desire and to be able to conquer self by renouncing our own will." Many other saints bear witness to this, St. Alphonsus Liguori, St. Aloysius Gonzaga, and St. Catherine of Siena, just to name a few. During their lifetimes, each one expressed their consummate desire to put aside personal possessions and earthly pleasures, family ties and physical comforts, so as to unite themselves wholly to Christ and His divine purpose for them. By detaching themselves from everything worldly and by identifying with the sufferings of Jesus, the saints soared to great spiritual heights. This may explain why so many of them struggled with a lack of physical health. It is as if they tacitly agreed to endure the pain, humiliation, and anguish that accompany chronically poor health in order to thoroughly defeat the demands of a personal will.

In more recent times, Pope and Saint John XXIII, who initiated the proceedings of Vatican II, had this to say early in his priestly career, "Once you have renounced everything, really everything, then any bold enterprise becomes the simplest and most natural thing in all the world!" (Quoted from "My Life with the Saints," originally from, "Wit and Wisdom of Good Pope John: Sayings Collected by Henri Fesquet,"1964). So how close are we to answering the ultimate question; can we "renounce everything, really everything?" Here "renounce" means letting go of our rightful claim to something, as the prophet Abraham did in his willingness to sacrifice his son Isaac. For more on this, see Lesson 8 in this series, "The Need for Obedience."

Back in the time of World War II, there lived an American Jesuit named Walter Ciszek, upon whose writings I often depend for insight and wisdom. He was arrested and sentenced to fourteen years imprisonment for the crime of being a Catholic priest. In his memoir, Fr. Ciszek recounts his ordeal, which he endured under the harshest conditions imaginable. The first four years of his sentence were spent in solitary confinement. Then he was relocated to do hard labor at a Soviet camp in northern Siberia. Under a brutal communist regime, Russia's "dissidents" were given no freedom at all. Despite the extreme deprivation he suffered, Fr. Ciszek writes, "The body can be confined, but nothing can destroy the deepest freedom in man, the freedom of the soul, and the freedom of the mind and will." Freedom in Christ Jesus is not only what kept this priest alive, but it is what gave him the strength to minister to his fellow prisoners in a spirit of total self-giving ("He Leadeth Me," by Walter Ciszek, S.J., 1973).

In conclusion, we come to realize that all of us face the same dilemma: How do we get through the trials of life with what amounts to sacrificial grace? And a second question is: Is it worth the price? Jesus tells us that we get through trials most efficaciously when we are in communion with like-minded souls, both living and deceased. The righteous souls who have died are referred to as, "The Communion of Saints," or as St. Paul calls them, "A Cloud of Witnesses." Paul's comments are found in Hebrews 12: 1: "Therefore, since we are surrounded by such a great cloud of witnesses, let us throw off everything that hinders and the sin that so easily entangles." This idea implies that those who have gone before us "surround us" from Heaven, providing spiritual help from above.

Then there are the "living saints" alive today, which include all true believers. These represent the universal Church and are called, "The Mystical Body of Christ." So although we receive aid from the saints in Heaven, we also align ourselves with the "saints" we encounter in daily life. When we do this, we actively participate in their sanctity, and we gain from them what we need to overcome our own personal struggles. Jesus tells us, "Whoever welcomes a prophet as a prophet will receive a prophet's reward, and whoever welcomes a righteous person as a righteous person will receive a righteous person's reward" (Matthew 10: 41). Does Jesus mean that we who recognize and respect a saintly person, and offer him or her whatever they need - be it encouragement, comfort, or financial support - will receive the same recompense? Yes! Whenever we assist good and righteous people, all those who sincerely try to follow the Will of God, or if we support the noble causes they champion, Jesus says we gain the same rich reward as is rightfully theirs.

This leads to the second question, "Is it worth it?" I refer to Matthew 19: 27, where the apostle Peter asks the same question. He exclaims, "See, we have left everything and followed you. What then will we have?" Jesus responds by making a promise to His disciples, assuring them that they will receive "a hundredfold, and shall inherit eternal life" (V 29). In giving our will over to a higher Power, we like Peter and like all the other saints, agree to accept whatever God wills for us. Then we too, are sustained by Jesus' awesome promise; your reward will be great in Heaven!

Me, a Saint?

In "My Life with the Saints," Fr. James Martin recounts a story about Thomas Merton. A conversation with Merton's friend takes place after he, Thomas, was baptized as an adult in 1938. During the exchange, the friend says, "What you should say is that you want to be a saint." Merton retorts, "How do you expect me to become a saint?" His friend replies, "By wanting to." Later, Merton pondered this thought and wrote, "For me to be a saint means for me to be myself." In other words, by being the one-of-a-kind person you are, and by aspiring to be the best version of that self you can be, you are on your way to sainthood, knowingly or not. To paraphrase Mother Teresa of Calcutta, everyone has a unique contribution to make, and no one else can do what you alone are able to do.

A Different Flock

In this essay, I speak directly to Christians. This is because we are under a special mandate to follow Christ ("The Imitation of Christ," by Thomas de Kempis, 1977). But if you are not Catholic, or not Christian; what then? Fortunately, there is reason to believe that all people of goodwill shall be united in glory. St. Peter exclaims: "I now realize how true it is that God does not show favoritism but accepts from every nation the one who fears Him and does what is right" (Acts 10: 34-35).

This perspective is defined in a document written in 1964 called, "Lumen Gentium." It is a treatise about a particular dogma of the Catholic Church, in which #16 addresses how we use our freewill and our hope for salvation. "Lumen Gentium" affirms that God honors ALL people who may not know Him but who, through their freewill choices, sincerely follow moral conscience and strive to preform good works. In other words, whether Muslim, Buddhist, Hindu, Jew, agnostic, or atheist, if people earnestly try to discipline themselves to do good and not to harm others, they too may receive eternal life through the sacrifice of Jesus Christ. When it is said, "Jesus died for everyone," this is precisely what is meant. Such an amazing promise is operative whether persons are aware of it or not, or even if they do not consciously believe it. This is a marvelous and prophetic vision! It suggests that a future unity is possible in which all cultures and nationalities will be open to God's grace. Perhaps this is what Jesus meant when He said, "I have other sheep also, which are not of this fold; them too, I must bring, and they will hear my voice; and all sheep will become one flock and there will be one shepherd" (John 10: 16). For a discussion about what this prophetic statement may portend for humanity, see the last Lesson in this series called, "End-Times Prophecy."

LESSON TWO

THE TRIUMPH OF

JUSTICE

THE TRIUMPH OF

JUSTICE

---

*"Behold, the days will come, says the Lord, that I
will raise unto David a righteous branch, and a King
shall reign and prosper, and shall execute judgment
and justice in the earth... and this is the Name
whereby He shall be called, 'The Lord of Justice"*

(Jeremiah 23: 5-6)

God's Intervention

When things go wrong, well-meaning people often resign themselves to a painful reality. They declare with certainty, "Everything happens for a reason, you know." Or a religious person might say, "It is God's Will." And although none of us can claim to understand "the why" of the evils that befall the world, perhaps it is easier to believe that somehow it was actually God who made the choice, and we justify this idea by saying what happened was meant for our benefit. If you are an atheist, you may believe it was simply Fate.

But if you insist that God was the reason for this or that happening, there is a problem with such a conviction. This is because it may or may not be true. And if we take it to its logical conclusion – the notion that God controls *everything* in our lives - we may be abdicating our freewill. In other words, by claiming that God absolutely governs what happens to mankind in the world, we cannot simultaneously acknowledge the power He gave us to choose for ourselves. And if freewill really doesn't exist, wouldn't God be some kind of Divine Overlord who pulls the strings of his puppet human beings from above? That is not a happy picture, and it is not one we profess as Christians. This topic is discussed in the previous Lesson, "The Evolution of Freewill."

On the other hand, it is also true that God directly intervenes in human affairs during certain periods in history, according to His most holy and perfect Will. In a particular gospel story, there is the case of the man born blind. Here Jesus states that this man's blindness had a preordained purpose. Before healing the blind man, "Jesus says to the crowd, 'Neither did he sin nor his parents (sin), but that the works of God might be seen in him." So at least in this instance, it appears the man's blindness was predetermined for a divine reason (John 9: 3). And of course, the premiere example of God's intervention in human affairs is the birth of His Son to a virgin named Mary. And we know that Jesus would die on the cross for our sins in order to accomplish the Will of the Father (John 17: 4).

Old Testament examples of God's intervention abound. They include God commanding Noah to build the Ark (Genesis 6: 8-14; 17-22), the birth of Isaac to Abraham and Sara (Genesis 21: 1-3), God granting Hezekiah, King of Judea, fifteen more years of life (Isaiah 38: 5), and most astonishing, God making time go backwards by reversing the movement of the sun (Isaiah 38: 8). These are just a few of many biblical narratives that reveal God's intervention in human affairs. Although such events seem rare today, they show we simply cannot say with certainty whether the divine Will has intervened in any given situation. What we can say is that at specific times, God does cause certain conditions or actions to occur in order to fulfill His inscrutable purposes.

But the age-old questions remain: why are some people born handicapped? Why are some born into wealth while others are consigned to poverty? There are good people everywhere whose lives end in tragedy. In the case of refugees, was it an accident of fate or God's intentional design that caused them to become victims of violence, human trafficking, and corruption? Many people have unrelenting physical problems, while others are the picture of health and vitality. Clearly, there is no level playing field in life.

On earth, Blessed Mother Mary must have dealt with this issue herself, not once but many times during the course of Jesus' life and ministry. Imagine her anguish when she came to the realization that her Son's life was spared at the expense of many parents whose infants were mercilessly murdered at the hands of Herod's henchmen (Matthew 2: 13-15). Obviously, God permitted this atrocious act of infanticide from which Jesus narrowly escaped. As already noted, we cannot presume to understand "the why" of it; all we can say is that God allowed it to happen. Nevertheless, I am sure the mother of Jesus suffered greatly in the aftermath of the killing of the Holy Innocents, pondering the horrific injustice that exists in the world, just as we ponder it today.

Mercy or Justice?

Jesus made a point to teach us not to demand justice in this life. In fact, He pretty much turned the tables on our conventional view of it. The parable of the Prodigal Son (Luke 15: 11-32) illustrates this point. Here God reveals Himself as a Merciful Father who gladly puts aside His lawful authority to judge His son's deviant behavior. Rather, the father lovingly embraces his son, offering him mercy and forgiveness. In another biblical story, the Woman Caught in Adultery (John 8: 1-11), civil and religious laws dictate that the woman should be stoned to death, but Jesus intervenes. Both narratives show that God's concept of fairness is not what the lawful authorities prescribe. To the contrary, in the eyes of God, love and compassion always preempt any legal authority. Furthermore, we are clearly instructed that the Heavenly Father, "makes His sun rise on the evil and the good and sends rain on the just and the unjust" (Matthew 5: 45). Such biblical verses suggest it is God's desire to withhold judgement, and they testify to the utmost importance of every human being, no matter how inadequate, weak, or rebellious they may be. For "a sparrow does not fall to the ground without your father's knowledge" (Matthew 10: 29).

God is aware of and concerned about everyone without exception!

How should we treat people who are unfair to us? In Hosea 6: 6, the Lord clearly states, "I desire mercy, and not sacrifice." The word "mercy" here means having compassion toward someone whom it is within our power to punish for wrongdoing. But to be Christ-like, we are asked to refrain from taking vengeful action which is rightfully (lawfully) ours to take. Doing this is more valuable to God than any sacrifice we can offer. Jesus comes right to the point: "If you forgive others of their transgressions, the Heavenly Father will forgive you, but if you do not forgive others, neither will your Father forgive your transgressions" (Matthew 6: 14-15).

It's Not Fair!

A passage from John 21: 22 illustrates what we interpret as a lack of fairness in the world. In this verse, Jesus speaks directly to the apostle Peter about John, saying, "If I want him to remain alive until I return, what is that to you?" It is as if Jesus is telling Peter (and us), "I am the Sovereign King, and if I wish to give a particular person an extraordinary gift, it is no concern of yours." The Lord bestows blessings on whomever He chooses.

The parable of the Laborers presents a situation which teaches the same lesson (Matthew 20: 1-16). Here we see the paradox of the employer paying the laborers who work only a fraction of the day, the same wages as those who work the entire day. This certainly goes against the grain. We say, "That's not fair!" However, when viewed from a spiritual angle, the story looks quite different. The benevolent Employer is our Heavenly Father, who offers those who wish to serve Him, the ultimate heavenly reward. The individuals who come to work early and chose to dedicate their day (that is, their entire lives) to His service, are given the pay which they rightfully deserve. But then the Employer, in His unfathomable generosity, freely decides to reward those who come to work late (that is, those who accept God's gift of salvation later in life) with exactly the same reward (that is, Heaven). This story points to the fact that God's gifts are offered gratis, without our having to "earn" them. Therefore, what is easily perceived as a lack of fairness in this story is actually an incredible gift. We who come late to serve Christ will receive the same reward as those who were there from the beginning and who never went astray. That's a wonderful promise!

Evil Exists in the World

When dealing with illness as well as countless other calamities that afflict humanity, it must be understood, evil does exist in the world. But evil, injustice, and the like are NOT the work of a benevolent Creator. The Congregation for the Doctrine of the Faith, a Catholic institution, looks at illness this way: "Although sickness may have positive consequences as a demonstration of the faithfulness of the just person, and for repairing the justice that is violated by sin, and also because it may cause a sinner to reform and set out on the way of conversion, it remains, however, an evil."

The biblical Book of Wisdom tells us, "God did not make death, nor does He rejoice in the destruction of the living. For He fashioned all things that they might have being; and the creatures of the world are wholesome, and there is not a destructive drug among them, nor (did He create) any domain of the netherworld on earth, for justice is undying" (Wisdom 1: 13-15). The Book further states, "For God formed man to be imperishable; the image of His own nature He made him. But by the envy of the devil, death entered the world, and they who belong to his company experience it" (Wisdom 2: 23-24). Ezekiel 18: 23 reveals God's thoughts: "Do you think I take pleasure in the death of the wicked, declares the Lord? Would not I prefer that he turn from his ways and live?'

These passages are meant to explain where evil originates and where God stands in all this. From them we conclude that the devil really does exist, and that all demonic influences originate from him. These ubiquitous influences create and perpetuate the wickedness, hatred, and injustices proliferating on earth in all their vainglory. For this reason, any anger you may feel toward God is misplaced. It is the devil's influence that inspires all destructive action and it is he who deserves your wrath. Our mission on earth is to help right the wrongs of the world, and to overcome the evil one, whom we recognize as the ultimate source of all suffering. Yes, God allows this situation to exist, but it is only to give us every possible opportunity to *finally* decide against evil and to leave it *completely* behind. In other words, if we turn away from wrongdoing once and for all, it is the same thing as devoting our lives to Jesus, for He is Goodness itself. Why do this? Because Jesus IS the only solution to evil, and really, He is the only viable option we have. The alternative is a nihilistic philosophy which can only result in despair.

When describing the appearance of the coming Messiah, the prophet Isaiah assures us that, "a bruised reed He shall not break, and a flickering lamp He shall not extinguish" (Isaiah 42: 3). In other words, the essence of the Divine Heart of Jesus is tender and loving, not wanting to snuff out the slightest hope and not wanting anyone to be lost. For our part, we must stay strong against all demonic forces by *standing strong in the authority of Jesus*. In doing so, we confidently and assertively renounce evil, and *by this same authority, command it to leave us*. God Himself gives us the ability and the power to do this through the blood sacrifice of the Perfect Lamb. Several essays in this series explore this topic. You will find aspects of it in Lesson 5, "Choose Life," and Lesson 8, "The Need for Obedience."

Justice Will Prevail

Once we internalize the biblical concept of justice, we realize that all things unfair are caused by the proliferation of evil which is allowed to exist, and which continues to exist apart from God. I must repeat, we can never fully comprehend the "why" of it. Nevertheless, we recognize the devil's only goal is to confound our desire to do what is right, and to highjack our feeble attempts at sanctity. Using the parable of the Seed, Jesus says as much: "Whoever hears the Word of the Kingdom and does not understand it, the evil one comes and snatches away the Word which has been sown in his heart" (Matthew 13: 19).

In the end though, we know the devil and his minions will be soundly defeated. Justice will prevail! Every subversive act ever committed will be subject to judgement, as declared long ago in the Wisdom Books of the Old Testament; I highlight some of the relevant passages in Lesson 13, "Gaining Wisdom." Many reassuring messages appear in the New Testament as well. We are told that perpetrators of evil and violence will be apprehended, since "every one of us will have to render an account of himself before God" (Romans 14: 12). In Luke 12: 2-3 we read: "There is nothing covered up that will not be revealed or hidden that will not be known. Accordingly, whatever you have said in the dark will be heard in the light, and what you have whispered in the inner rooms will be proclaimed upon the housetops." For countless oppressed people who cry out against unbridled treachery and greed, these Scriptures promise justice. Someday, those whose nefarious acts have escaped detection and who "have gotten away with murder," will be exposed and dealt with by a just God.

Romans 8: 28-29 gives more encouraging news: "We know all things work together for good to them that love God, to them who are called according to His purpose." Therefore, since we are called to follow Him, God promises to mitigate the effects of evil in our lives. He "steps in" when we plea for help, and He will not allow the evil that surrounds us in the world to overtake us. Psalm 1: 6 assures, "The Lord watches over the way of the just, but the way of the wicked shall perish." We truly have a loving Heavenly Father!

People everywhere should welcome this revelation with deep consolation and immense joy, knowing that justice will ultimately triumph in the Kingdom of God! Psalm 47: 10 proclaims the day we will shout for joy, for "Your Name, O God, like Your praise, will reach to the ends of the earth; Your right hand is full of righteousness." When that day dawns, "He will wipe every tear from their eyes. There will be no more death or mourning or crying or pain, for the old order of things will have passed away" (Revelation 21: 4).

LESSON THREE

TRUE

ABUNDANCE

TRUE ABUNDANCE

" I did the planting, and Apollos the watering, but it was God who made the plants grow."

(1 Corinthians 3: 6)

The Principle of Loaves and Fishes

Do you sometimes marvel at how certain things seem to fall into place without any effort on your part? Have you ever found unexpected cash in your wallet, wondering how it got there? Does your garden produce so much surplus food that you can't give it away fast enough? Do your resources "multiply" in such a way that you are at a loss to explain it? These things have happened to me often enough, to the point where I coined a phrase to describe it: "The Principle of Loaves and Fishes."

I will offer a personal story which illustrates abundance and how it works. Dining at a restaurant one day, my husband and I were astonished to be seated by a very rude waitress. Her demeanor was sour, her service poor, and her attitude was offensive. We talked at length during the meal about her rudeness, deciding indignantly she would receive no tip from us!

But then I suggested that maybe she was just having a bad day, maybe her children were sick and she was the only breadwinner in the family. As we explored several, reasonable possibilities, we decided to reverse our decision, speculating that by giving the waitress a really BIG tip, it might change her attitude. Lo and behold, it worked! She gave us a 20% discount coupon on the spot, and when we returned some time later, she greeted us with a huge smile. Her service and care were excellent. A cynic might say this was all a charade staged for our benefit, with the hope of collecting another big tip. But no - in time we observed that this waitress' attitude really had changed. We were amazed that the transformation was not only real but it was lasting!

The ability to give and receive the incredible bounty of God's graces and blessings in routine, everyday circumstances is what "The Principle of Loaves and Fishes" is all about. Didn't Jesus say, "If your faith is the size of a mustard seed you will say to this mountain, 'Move from here to there, and it will move; nothing will be impossible for you' " (Matthew 17: 20)? Although we may be far from mastering a spirituality as elevated as "the faith that moves mountains," Jesus encourages us to begin, to start somewhere. I started by affirming and accepting the truth of His words and actions. That done, I wanted to know the actual circumstances of how the multiplication of Loaves and Fishes took place, and so I went to my Bible to find out.

The Multiplication

In the Old Testament, there is an account in which the prophet Elisha multiplies barley loaves to feed a hundred people (1 Kings 4: 42-44). In the New Testament, each of the four Evangelists (Matthew, Mark, Luke, and John) records a new version of the story. This time it is Jesus who feeds the hungry crowd; there are 5000 men present (not counting the women and children who were there). Also, Matthew and Mark describe a second occasion where Jesus feeds 4000 people. For convenience, I will stick mainly to Matthew's Gospel to describe the circumstances. In Chapter 14: 13 -16, we see Jesus going alone into the boat to pray, but many people have followed Him on land. When He saw the huge crowd, He left the boat and came ashore to heal the people. In the evening, the disciples asked Jesus about dismissing the crowd, "to buy food for themselves," for there was nothing to eat. But Jesus' response was unexpected; He said, "Give them something to eat yourselves."

By throwing the problem back into the disciples' lap, Jesus was saying, "You can handle this without my help." Was He simply testing their faith? In John's version of the story, it says Jesus definitely was (John 6: 6). But either way, it is clear the disciples felt totally unprepared and incapable of meeting such a challenge. They had almost no resources and were asked to provide food for a huge multitude of people; this was Mission Impossible for them. "We have nothing here except five loaves of bread and 2 fish!" they exclaimed (Matthew 14:17)

At this moment, Jesus was teaching the disciples (and also us) about how "The Principle of Loaves and Fishes" works:

Lesson #1 - Do not be afraid. Be willing to make use of what you have on hand, no matter how small it is. And Lesson #2 - Be prepared to unselfishly offer and share whatever you have with those in need.

Going back to Matthew 13: 8 - 9, we find the parable of the Sower. "Still other seeds fell on good soil and produced a crop — a hundredfold, sixtyfold, or thirtyfold. He who has ears, let him hear." In this passage, Jesus confirms that the multiplication will take place, as surely as good seed germinates, sprouts, grows to maturity, and yields abundant fruit. So Lesson #3 is - Maintain total confidence that what you have freely given will be multiplied.

Luke 8: 15 says, "When they have heard the Word, they hold fast to it, and yield a harvest through their perseverance." Let's compare this verse with the parable of the Farmer: "Night and day he sleeps and wakes, and the seed sprouts and grows, though he knows not how. All by itself the soil produces grain, first the stalk, then the head, then the full kernel in the head. As soon as the grain is ripe, he puts the sickle to it, because the harvest has come." (Mark 4: 26-29). What these two passages have in common is they both convey the need for confident and patient waiting until the harvest is ready.

So Lesson #4 is - Be willing to wait as the farmer waits for the seed he planted to grow to full maturity. Then you can expect an abundant crop, one that is reaped "through perseverance." Like the farmer, we do not know how the multiplication takes place, but when it does, the results can be truly miraculous!

Lastly, there is a final lesson contained in verse 20 of Matthew 14. It speaks about what happened after the miraculous multiplication of the Loaves and Fishes took place. "Everyone ate and had enough. Then the disciples took up twelve baskets full of what was left over." <u>Lesson #5</u> is - Do not to waste a single drop of what God has provided.

Human Frailty

In the following sequence of Matthew 14, Jesus tells the disciples to get into the boat without Him. They must set out for the other side (V 21 – 22). Now the Sea of Galilee is quite large, and sudden gales can arise out of nowhere. Furthermore, this time of evening is especially vulnerable, for it is the time when violent storms suddenly erupt on the sea. Surely the disciples knew this. We can only imagine their trepidation as they got into the boat and headed out on their own. Was Jesus testing their faith again?

"After He sent them away, He went up on the mountain by Himself to pray....but the boat was already far from land, buffeted by the waves because the wind was against it" (V 24). "And in the fourth watch of the night, Jesus came to them walking on the water. When the disciples saw Him, they were terrified...and they cried out in fear. Immediately Jesus spoke to them, saying, 'Take courage, it is I; do not be afraid'" (V 25-27). Then at the apostle Peter's request, Jesus bade him to come and walk on the water to Him. (V 28-29). Peter started out, but when the wind whipped up and the sea howled, he lost his nerve and began to sink (V 30). Peter must have looked away and taken his eyes off of the One who can save us all. Fortunately, as soon as he got into deep trouble, Peter cried out to the Lord, who immediately reached out and rescued him (V 31).

Three Essential Virtues

The story above illustrates the frailty of human nature. First of all, it shows we must have Courage just to begin to confront the obstacles that beset us. Secondly, no matter how steadfast and self-assured we are, our resolve is only as good as the Faith and Trust we place in the Lord. Revisiting this biblical story, we will accompany St. Peter, this time using a few metaphors along the way, in order to experience the account as it directly relates to us.

Let's say that the boat, being tossed about by the waves at

the mercy of the sea, is us! And it also represents the precariousness of the human condition. Remember, "The wind was against it" (Matthew 14: 24). Peter, finding the nerve to leave the relative safety of the boat, is like the person who "steps out in faith." So we, like Peter, must decide to exit our "safe zone." At first, we observe a courageous Peter who is able to muster enough resolve to get out of the boat, which as I said, is an aspect of ourselves. In fact, leaving the boat is an attempt "to get out of ourselves," or our former way of life. Like St. Peter, we may eagerly decide to exit the boat, thinking only of Jesus' invitation to "Come!" But then, we find ourselves "in the water," buffeted by an angry and violent sea, which represents everything that tries to unsettle us. Here, it is only our faith and trust which enable us to survive. Those virtues sustain us in the rigors of the colossal effort it takes to stay afloat; and ultimately, they get us past the barriers that are blocking our way. Just as in the story, we must never take our eyes off Jesus, or like Peter, we will surely sink. Fortunately, this biblical narrative assures us that Jesus is always right there to grab us should we falter.

True Abundance

Applying the simple truths which Jesus taught is the surest path to success. In this brief essay, I have outlined His instructions which I describe as, "The Principle of Loaves and Fishes." First, I show how following Five Lessons from Scripture will reap a multiplication of resources. Then, St. Peter's story teaches the need for "The Three Essential Virtues" of courage, faith, and trust. These spiritual qualities must lead the way when we are feeling weak or incapable, or when we are experiencing loss or deprivation. Together, they provide the key which unlocks the door to God's unimaginable graces and blessings, paving the way to nothing less than "True Abundance." Correctly applied, these same attributes empower us to focus our physical and spiritual energies, multiplying whatever meager resources we may have at our disposal.

Remember, the twenty-third Psalm declares that Jesus takes care of all our needs. But as we have seen, He also offers so much more; His magnificent bounty, which is the multiplication of the Loaves and Fishes in our lives!

LESSON FOUR

A BIBLICAL STORY OF

HEALING

A BIBLICAL STORY OF

HEALING

" But unto you that fear My Name shall the Son of righteousness arise with Healing in His wings."

(Malachi 4: 2)

Do You Want to Be Healed?

Jesus once asked this question to a man suffering a physical disability whom He had observed at the Pool of Bethsaida (John 5: 4-9). In the story, we are told that because of the severity of his infirmity, the man was unable to get to the pool and lower himself into its healing waters. For thirty-eight long years, he endured this humiliation without relief, so you might think that Jesus's question, "Do you want to be healed?" was a bit out of line. "Of course, I want to be healed!" you would expect the man to exclaim! But apparently, Jesus thought otherwise.

There is more to this Gospel story than meet the eye, and it is instructive to look deeper. Let's explore why Jesus might have asked this question in the first place. And we will look at its relevance for us today.

Imagine being crippled, waiting at the Pool of Bethsaida for thirty-eight years for a cure that never came. In the narrative, we are told that healing occurred there only at certain times, when an angel of the Lord came down into the pool, stirring the waters. Then, the first to go down into the pool would be "cured of whatever infirmity he had." (John 5: 4). Can you imagine the frustration the man in the story experienced time after time, finding himself completely unable to reach the healing waters of the pool in time? We know from the narrative that someone always got there ahead of him, before he even had a chance. (V 7).

Surely at some point, the man came to accept the fact that he would never be cured of his disability from the waters of the pool. In resigning himself to this belief, it is easy to understand why he probably had neither the faith nor the inclination to keep on trying. Over time, we can even speculate that the man had become accustomed to his way of life and had adapted to it fairly well. Perhaps he was making a good living as a beggar, and that occupation was all he knew or was able to do. It is also possible that the man might have felt too lazy on that particular day to exert the energy required to get himself down into the healing waters one more time. His attitude may well have been, "Really? Why should I even bother trying?"

Whatever the man's thoughts were, Jesus knew them, and this is precisely why He asked him, "Do you want to be healed?" Can you picture Jesus standing there in front of the man saying something like this: "I am about to transform your life. Are you really ready for a drastic and radical change from the lifestyle you have grown accustomed to?"

So too, for us. Ask yourself: "Could I accept the new life that a cure would require?" When looking for healing from the Lord, we face the same question today as did the man at the Pool of Bethsaida so long ago: "Do I *really* want to be healed?"

After deciding, "Yes, I truly want the cure," there are still two questions to answer: First, "Do I really believe that I *can* be cured?" Secondly, "Do I really believe that Jesus *will* do it?" In other words, do I take Him at His word and do I fully trust in His promises? These questions present the ultimate challenge, for they require that we believe with all our heart, despite the fact that there may be no immediate or apparent results. It is also likely we will still face difficulties, disappointments, feelings of rejection, and perhaps even bouts of depression in the course of our lives. Despite all these things, "Do I *still* believe a cure is possible?"

In studying the story of the man at the Pool of Bethsaida, we can gain some insight into how we should approach the entire question of healing. We may also discover why many of us are not cured, even though we are sincere in our prayer request. This story reveals some possible answers, which I call the "Five Conditions."

Five Conditions

Faith: Like the man at the pool, it is difficult indeed to keep on believing. When we face trials, our struggles can easily lead us to cynicism and doubt. Yet Jesus insists that when it comes to healing, faith is essential (Luke 7: 50). The only solution for our lack of faith lies in our consciously cultivating, nurturing, and renewing a robust and abiding faith, one that can withstand the onslaught of the uncertainties and setbacks which we all experience in life.

Patience: There is no doubt that the man at the Pool of

Bethsaida had patience. But he waited and waited in vain. His incredible patience may have been the thing that drew Jesus to him, since Jesus chose this particular man out of "a great multitude of the sick, blind, lame, and those with shriveled limbs, (who were) waiting for the stirring of the waters." (John 5: 3) In endless waiting, both our patience and faith are sorely tested. I wonder how many of us would steadfastly wait for a cure anywhere near as long as the man at the pool did!

Proximity to a Healing Place: As shown in this gospel story, there were then, and are today, places in the world with special healing significance; Fatima and Lourdes come to mind. Closer to home, our local churches are places where healing takes place, and healing prayer services offer a special opportunity to obtain the graces we wish to receive through the power of the Holy Spirit. We must take full advantage of our very own Healing Place, our local church.

Encounter with God: Jesus dispensed with the use of the healing waters at the Pool of Bethsaida by curing the man who was crippled in a direct, dramatic, and spontaneous fashion, saying, "Rise, take up your pallet, and walk" (V 8). Our encounter with Jesus has to be just as close, just as immediate, and just as personal. Intimacy with Him is achieved through fervent prayer and meditation. It is attained most effectively when we receive Jesus in Holy Communion with deep reverence and love.

Freedom from Sin: After the cure, the narrative reveals that Jesus slipped quietly away (V 13). However, later on, Jesus found the man in the temple and said to him, "Behold, you are cured. Sin no more, lest something worse befall you" (V 14). Jesus' statement suggests that if we persist in sin, we may relapse into our former condition, or worse. The remedy of course, is to remain perpetually in God's grace, that we might enjoy all the blessings which He lovingly wishes to bestow on us.

Examining Jesus' words further, we recognize that the final ingredient in the healing recipe involves our attitude. Understandably, after waiting at the Pool of Bethsaida for thirty-eight long years without a cure, the crippled man may have built up some powerfully negative feelings! Perhaps he felt resentment, bitterness, or unforgiveness. The story suggests that indeed he did. Otherwise, why would Jesus make it a point later to tell him, "Sin no more"? One thing for sure, unless we are able to conquer the angry or judgmental thoughts we harbor against ourselves or others, we will not receive what we ask for in prayer.

So whether we request healing for a particular situation or problem, or even if we ask for a physical cure, Jesus has given us specific guidelines to follow. Through His treatment of the man at the Pool of Bethsaida, we learn what is required of those who seek solace and relief from the demands and hardships of life. As faith-filled followers of Christ, the Healer, we dare to approach the Throne of grace and mercy.

LESSON FIVE

CHOOSE

LIFE

CHOOSE LIFE

" I am the Resurrection and the Life; whoever believes in me, even if he dies, will live, and anyone who lives and believes in me will never die."

(John 11: 19-20)

You Must Choose

There is an often-quoted passage from the Old Testament which has to do with the timeless question of Life vs. Death. It is found in the Book of Deuteronomy, Chapter 30: 15-19:

See, I have set before you this day life and good, and death and evil. In that I command you this day to love the Lord your God, to walk in His ways, and to keep His commandments and His statutes and His judgments, that you may live and multiply, and the Lord your God shall bless you in the land whither you go to possess it.

But if your heart turn away, so that you will not

hear, but shall be drawn away, and worship other gods, and serve them. I denounce unto you this day, that you shall surely perish, and that you shall not prolong your days upon the land, when you pass over Jordan to go to possess it.

I call heaven and earth to record this day, that I have set before your life and death, blessing and cursing therefore, choose life, that both you and your seed may live.

A Curse or a Blessing?

The same dualism we recognize in the above passage from Deuteronomy, has existed throughout recorded time: Black or white, night or day, evil or good, a curse or a blessing, death or life. In modern times, these dualistic concepts have crystalized into archetypal images as they relate to our dynamic understanding of consciousness. These ideas were thoroughly articulated in the works of Joseph Campbell and Carl Jung. However, long before that, the ancient Chinese Taoist symbol of Yin/Yang embodied the same timeless message, and we see this symbol today as a popular representation of the pairing of opposites. Yet, when we view opposites from the vantage point of archetypes, it seems that most of us would greatly prefer to avoid "darkness," since symbolically, it represents corruption and evil. However, we know there are many people today who do not share this attitude. Instead, they eagerly gravitate to "the dark side" and turn away from "the light." I am sure there are a multitude of reasons for making this choice, but I will only speculate on a few of them here.

The Generational Curse

We can look at life as a precious gift from the Creator. And the Bible always encourages us to choose upright, affirmative actions, so as to bring about an abundance of blessings, rather than a curse, upon us. But if we don't actively pursue this life-giving mindset, both as individuals and as a nation, we invite calamity. I say this because of what is known as, the "Generational Curse," whose existence may account for some of the many ills which afflict society today. Make no mistake, the "Generational Curse" is a very real thing. The most famous example of it is observed in the family history of the Kennedy clan ("The Kennedy Curse: Why Tragedy Has Haunted America's First Family for 150 Years," by Edward Klein). Unfortunately, for ordinary families, the curse is equally real. Just ask those who suffer the lingering effects of domestic violence, mental illness, genetic defects and diseases, suicide, chronic drug and alcohol addictions, homelessness, as well as any number of perversions which repeat from one generation to the next. In the Old Testament, God commands, "You shall not bow down yourself unto them, nor serve them (false gods); for I, the Lord your God, am a jealous God, visiting the iniquity of the fathers upon the children unto the third and fourth generation of them that hate Me" (Deuteronomy 5: 9). Here the Lord clearly states that there are awful consequences for those who choose to deny, insult, or hate Him, *and these consequences are passed down to their offspring for several generations.* Contrast this with Jesus' life-affirming statement recorded in the New Testament: "I have come that they might have life, and that they might have it more abundantly" (John 10: 10). Can the choice be any clearer? Because of His immense love, Jesus declares His desire to release humanity from the grip of all generational curses. It is only with and through Him that we can cleanse and redeem our bloodline. But this redemptive gift is mostly rejected by those who need it the most, and so the "Generational Curse" remains one of the most lethal afflictions that has yet to be conquered. Perhaps a complete cure from this malady cannot happen for families until society as a whole addresses the peripheral issues which perpetuate the curse, such as racial strife, bigotry, violence, chronic poverty, food insecurity, and an unjust legal system.

What is pertinent to this discussion is the question: Do the small decisions we make today, every single day, have real, long-term impact, maybe even for generations to come? Is every choice, from the most insignificant to the largest, truly a "Life or Death" matter? You may scoff at such an idea. For example, you may think the Bible's references to "idol worship," or worshipping "false gods," is a thing of the past. But I invite you to think again. We cannot settle the issue unless we revisit Deuteronomy 30, especially verse 17. Here I want to consider the words, "worship other gods and serve them." Perhaps the modern interpretation of this phrase can shed light on this matter.

The Golden Calf

First, let's look at who were those "other gods" of long ago mentioned in Deuteronomy. During the time of Moses, it is apparent that one of them was the golden calf described in

Exodus 32: 1-4. "When the people saw that Moses was so long in coming down from the mountain, they gathered around Aaron and said, "Come, make us gods who will go before us. As for this fellow Moses who brought us up out of Egypt, we don't know what has happened to him." Let me point out here that the Israelites' patience finally wore out. After all, they had grown weary from the deprivation they had suffered ever since fleeing Egypt. I guess their angst reached its apex when Moses did not return to camp. In order to appease the people, Aaron answered, 'Take off the gold earrings that your wives, your sons and your daughters are wearing, and bring them to me.' So, all the people took off their earrings and brought them to Aaron. He took what they handed him and made it into an idol cast in the shape of a calf, fashioning it with a tool." Then they said, 'These are your gods Israel, who brought you up out of Egypt.'

Why did the Israelites, the self-professed, chosen people of God among the nations, prefer the obviously, man-made idol of a golden calf over the one, true God? It seems absurd to us today! As noted above, I believe the Israelites became so irked when Moses did not return quickly, they felt they had to manufacture something "significant" to fill the void.

Certainly, their lack of patience made them unwilling to "wait on the Lord," as the psalmist declares in Psalm 130. On the other hand, St. Peter tells us, "The Lord does not delay concerning His promises, as some count delay, but is longsuffering toward us, not willing that any should perish but that all should come to repentance" (2 Peter 3: 9). This statement presents a strange paradox: It suggests that it was actually God who was being patient with the Israelites, and not the other way around! But ironically, it seems God's patience tried theirs to the breaking point! So I suspect one solution to the problem of "idol worship" that we see all around us today, centers around the quality we call patience.

Learning to Wait

No doubt, one of the biggest obstacles in modern society is the inability to wait. And yes, this is no small matter. In Luke's Gospel, Chapter 21: 19, we read, "In your patience, you possess your soul." Today, a chronic lack of patience is at the core of many rash decisions, especially in our Western culture. That's why occurrences such as road rage and car-jacking have become common place. I also suspect the recent proliferation of mass shootings is fueled, at least in part, by a growing lack of both patience and tolerance. Violence is the outcome of a rage that is allowed to simmer over time, has no positive outlet, and finally explodes. For rage to foment in a person's heart, the virtuous qualities of serenity and patience must be entirely absent from them.

There is another problem of waiting which is widespread today, and for most, it is exceedingly difficult to endure; it is the decision for chastity until marriage. In other words, pre-marital sex can be seen as a reflection of our impatience, of our inability to wait. And as tragic as it is, a lack of patience may also be a factor in the decision to end an unwanted pregnancy. A woman facing a nine-month hiatus from her normal routine may see it as a huge inconvenience, an inconvenience she literally cannot afford. Beyond that, in cases where the mother is bereft of support, she must exert tremendous fortitude and patience just to carry the baby to term. After delivery, she may fear the prospect of nurturing and raising a dependent, unwanted child. During the best of circumstances, all good parents know that parenthood takes plenty of time and patience, with both parents actively participating. The prospect of doing this formidable task alone must be daunting.

The use of euthanasia in the dying process gives another

clue about what may be seen as a patience issue. With no hope of recovery, the suffering person chooses to bring about his own death rather than prolong his agony. He simply cannot bear to suffer any longer and, knowing that his family suffers along with him, he wants to relieve their pain as well. For the family, a difficult and prolonged illness can only add to their grief (and their medical bills). This is a heart-wrenching situation for sure. However, there is ample biblical evidence that all suffering can be redemptive, and I might add, necessary "to work out our salvation with fear and trembling" (Philippians 2: 12). For many who are looking for an opportune exit, this is a hard pill to swallow (no pun intended).

To put it another way, the so called, "right to die" movement completely misses the point because it does not see a protracted death as an opportunity for spiritual growth. That's where Hospice plays a vital role. Hospice offers all the comforts available in modern medicine to the dying patient, but his final days are not deliberately cut short. From a Christian point of view, ending a life prematurely denies the person the chance to offer his or her life and death as a gift, a gift one willingly gives to the Heavenly Father. Such a gift is pleasing to Him, and it greatly benefits the person, as well as those who love and care for him.

Another form of practicing patience is found in prayer. When we try to listen to God, we often get impatient and distracted, because we do not sense a tangible response from Him. Yet God *is* responding, but we must wait for the "ripening" of our own spiritual maturation so that we are able to discern God's voice. For more on this, see the next Lesson, "Heart-felt Prayer."

As a result of today's fast-paced culture, I conclude that the virtue of patience is one which many men and women lack and no longer value. By the way, this includes how we judge ourselves. Yes, we must remember to be patient with ourselves too, not just with one another. It is not enough that we don't put others down for their mistakes, if we then put ourselves down for the little (and big), sometimes stupid mistakes we make! In order to cultivate patience, we must stop doing that.

Biblical Idols and Other gods

The Bible mentions "other gods" whose identities are revealed in parables and stories from both the Old and New

Testaments. Jealousy, greed, envy, lust, gluttony, drunkenness, and the quest for power, seem to be reoccurring themes. Well-known stories from the Old Testament illustrate over and over again, man's defiance of God's Law. These stories include Cain and Abel, Joseph, Esther, Ruth, King Saul, and many others. Each one portrays a path of destruction brought about by those who seek treachery and self-aggrandizement above all else. These then, have become their gods. And of course, other characters in the Old Testament chose to directly engage in pagan idol worship. We see parallels today in the practices of witchcraft and Satanism.

Ezekiel 8 tells of a vision the prophet had, where atrocities committed by Israel had become so appalling that the only cure was to purge the nation of its evil doers. These ancient Israelites, chosen by God to be His people, deliberately and woefully disregarded what the Lord had asked of them. Despite the many prophetic warnings, they had received, they persisted in pursuing their corrupt practices, that is, their "idols," which they "worshipped" in thought and deed. In this biblical passage from Ezekiel, these idols are called, "wicked abominations."

Jealousy and lust were singled out as especially egregious, but there must have been other transgressions besides these. In verse 17, Ezekiel says, "Then He said unto me, 'Hast thou seen this, O son of man? Is it a light thing to the house of Judah that they commit the abominations which they commit here? For they have filled the land with violence, and have returned to provoke me to anger.' "

Bad Thoughts

In the New Testament, there are similar warnings. The main difference though, is that the list of offenses has expanded to include one's very thoughts. "Jesus came not to abolish the Law, but to fulfill it" (Matthew 5: 17). He wants us to know the things that lead to Life, and what leads to Death. Accordingly, He preached a new Gospel, stating that even thinking erroneous thoughts is wrong and constitutes a transgression. Most of us recall His famous admonition about how lusting after a woman in your heart is sinful (Matthew 5: 28). That's because doing this is, in a real sense, a form of idol worship. Furthermore, lust can turn into the addiction which is so prevalent today - pornography. The truth is, excessively dwelling on any impure or licentious thought produces idolatry, or "serving other gods," or choosing death over the life of the soul.

The remedy to Jesus' stark declaration concerning aberrant thoughts, is that we must surrender our problematic urges, preferences, and behaviors to Him, in order to make room for enlightened, more noble thoughts and actions. Jesus explains this to the woman at the well when He says to her: "But the hour is coming, and now is, when the true worshipers shall worship the Father in spirit and truth, for the Father seeks such to worship Him" (John 4:23). Therefore, if we truly honor God as the Lord and Savior of our lives, our self-centered thoughts and deeds must eventually fall away, so we can be open and receptive to the Divine Word. That is when we will worship God in "Spirit and Truth."

Jesus is vehement about this. "If your eye causes you to sin, pluck it out..." (Matthew 18: 9). Obviously, Jesus does not mean this literally, but He wants us to get the point. We must aggressively eradicate errant thoughts and deeds from our consciousness and replace them with spiritual promptings inspired by God. Man's proper worship will occur only when this takes place in the individual and in the world at large. When it does, peace will reign! (See Lesson 17, "End-Times Prophecy").

66

Likewise, after St. Paul was purified in thought and deed, he joyfully exclaims, "It is no longer I who live, but Christ living in me!" (Galatians 2: 19-21). And Jesus Himself tells us, "I am the vine, you are the branches.... without Me you can do nothing" (John 15: 5). Fr. Paul Murray, a contemporary Dominican priest on YouTube, combines these two ideas and puts them into one sentence when he says simply, "Jesus wants to live His Life in you."

In 1 Corinthians 5: 8, St. Paul muses about death. If we should die, he concludes, "We are confident, I say, and willing rather to be absent from the body, and to be present with the Lord." Paul plainly states that by choosing wisely now and throughout our lifetime, physical death will be swallowed up in a new life, a life that is eternal. He assures us that either way, we are in the hands of our Heavenly Father. "If we live, we live for the Lord; and if we die, we die for the Lord. So, whether we live or die, we belong to the Lord" (Romans 14: 8). St. Paul could make this bold assertion because he understood the profound implications of Jesus's words: "For just as the Father raises the dead and gives them life, even so the Son gives life to those whom He will" (John 5: 21). Thus, our very life, our entire existence, whether as living creatures on earth or as eternal citizens in Heaven, depends upon Jesus sustaining us with His very own Life.

Modern gods

In today's world, there are too many false gods to name more than a few of them in this short essay, but you know who they are. Besides the classic, biblical vices highlighted above, corruption and wickedness brought about by excessive wealth, fame, and material success are the most common ones we see today.

There is also the specter of white supremacy and nationalism gaining ground as an ideological, social value. Are these things poised to become the new gods of our hedonistic culture? Meanwhile, teens and young adults play video games, ad nauseam, and a good number of them contain demonic content. In fact, all electronic devices have one thing in common; they conveniently "fill the void" in our lives so perfectly! To the extent that they do this, they may qualify as "other gods," not unlike the golden calf the Israelites occupied their time constructing while waiting for Moses' return. To restate what I said earlier, if fanatical behavior or extreme immoderation are allowed to creep into our consciousness, take over our daily lives, or negatively impact our moral judgement, they can be considered "false gods" or "idols."

Woke Culture

Wikipedia provides a working framework for what this new ideology is all about. Its beginnings were planted in our culture about ten years ago:

> The term "woke" gained popularity amid an increasing leftward turn on various issues among the American Left; this was partly a reaction to the right-wing politics of US President Donald Trump, who was elected in 2016, but also by a growing awareness regarding the extent of historical discrimination faced by African Americans. Ideas that came to be associated with "woke" included a rejection of American exceptionalism; a belief that the United States has never been a true democracy; that people of color suffer from systemic and institutional racism; that white Americans experience white privilege…"

Since its inception, Woke Culture has steadily grown to embrace a socialist and Marxist creed. Today, the term

"Woke" is used to denote the entire array of extreme, left-wing political movements, perspectives, and ideologies, especially those which emphasize identity politics, the plight of people of color, the LGBT community, and women. At its heart, it is anti-religious. Conversely, some observers of our contemporary culture believe the movement qualifies as a new, false religion ("Bishop Robert Barron Presents: Conversations at the Crossroads," August 2021).

Science

Another strong contender in the vast field of modern "idol worship, "is science. According to Italian philosopher Augusto Del Noce (1910-1989), "Scientism is the reigning religion of our time." This seems to be true; in our culture we have elevated science and technology to godlike status. And as long as the sciences refuse to take classic spiritual tenets seriously, sharing the stage as an equal, true, and essential partner in the quest for knowledge and meaning, science will remain just what it is today, an idol. For more on this topic, I suggest Lesson 9, "Finding Truth."

Sacramental Life

Following the prescriptions that lead to life is a good

strategy, but let's return to what Jesus means when He says He alone offers abundant Life. The answer is found in the classic work, "He Leadeth Me." I highlight the author's reflection on the sacraments in which we Christians partake, particularly baptism, which Fr. Ciszek calls, "The sacrament of the Life of faith." He believes baptism imparts the abundant Life of which Jesus speaks; it bestows a transcendent, supernatural quality that must be "nurtured and preserved for all eternity." Beyond baptismal Life, Fr. Ciszek claims that all the holy sacraments produces a supernatural Vitality, even in the most spiritually barren places and in the cruelest of conditions. The priest experienced this first-hand in the brutal communist system under which he labored and which he so vividly portrays in his book ("He Leadeth Me," by Fr. Walter Ciszek, 1973).

A Prediction

At the time of Fr. Ciszek's frightful ordeal, the communist government was particularly ruthless, and it strictly forbade all priests from saying Mass or administering the sacraments under penalty of death. Fr. Ciszek did so in secret. He pressed on, believing wholeheartedly that God would provide for him. And he witnessed a remarkable, vibrant, "underground" faith among the Russian people, a faith that remained unshaken despite constant threats and persecution by the totalitarian regime. The author concludes, "No one knows better than those who are constantly attacking the faith how firmly its seed remains planted in Russia; only God in His providence knows how soon it will flower." Was he predicting a time when new Life will spring forth in a bourgeoning, faith-filled populace? This could happen since at Fatima, Portugal in 1917, the Blessed Virgin Mary predicted the conversion of Russia. Did Fr. Ciszek actually foresee this future event? I believe he did.

LESSON SIX

HEART-FELT

PRAYER

HEART-FELT PRAYER

" The Proper place for the heart of a human being
is the heart of God"

(St. Augustine)

Understanding the Heart

D o you know how many times the word "heart" is mentioned in the Bible? The number varies somewhat depending on which translation you choose, but the word appears an astounding 762 times, plus another 114 if you count the plural, "hearts!" I think this discovery calls for a closer look at one of the Bible's most prominent, essential, and thought-provoking words.

You might ask, "What does the word "heart" in Scripture have to do with prayer?" St. Therese of Lisieux, the Little Flower, once remarked, 'For me, prayer is the heart's impulse, a simple gaze toward heaven. It is a cry of gratitude and love, from the depths of trial as well as the heights of joy" (quoted from her autobiography, "The Story of a Soul"). So, as the Little Flower teaches, the heart takes center stage in prayer. As we look deeper, we also find out how the heart and mind are connected, both of them referred to as one thing in the Bible, simply "the heart." Working in unison, the heart and mind produce the need and the desire to pray. Lastly, we will discover how all three elements, heart, mind, and prayer, ultimately connect us to the transcendent nature of the Divine. We cannot pray effectively unless we become aware of this interconnection. Because we first need an understanding of the Heart of God, we will start there. You will soon discover a loving Creator who is quite literally, "All Heart."

Who Is God?

Fortunately, both the Old and New Testaments are replete with descriptions that reveal God's fundamental nature. Let me mention a number of passages here: God is Holy (Isaiah 6: 3; 1 Peter 1: 16), Generous (Proverbs 19: 17; Luke 6: 38), and Responsive to our needs (Philippians 4: 19; Romans 8: 23). He is All-forgiving (1 John 1: 9; Acts 10: 43), Truthful (Proverbs 12: 22; John 17: 17), and Trustworthy (Hebrews 6: 18; Romans 4: 20-21). God is portrayed as Goodness itself (Deuteronomy 32: 4; 1 Corinthians 13: 4-6). He is Pure (1 John 3: 3; Psalm 12: 6) and Humble (James 4: 6; Matthew 11: 29). God commands us to Serve others (Mark 9: 35; 2 Timothy 4: 5). He is Abba, an affectionate term for Father, which conveys an intimate, caring, and paternal relationship. God is described as Presence (Mark 14: 36; Galatians 4: 6), and St. John identifies Him as Love, for "He who does not love does not know God, for God is love" (1 John 4: 8).

But God also speaks of Himself as a Jealous God, and He insists that His people love Him first and foremost (Exodus 20: 5). Likewise, no one can deny that God has a vengeful side: "The Lord is vengeful and strong in wrath. The Lord is vengeful against His foes; He rages against His enemies. The Lord is very patient but great in power; the Lord punishes...Who can stand before his indignation?" (Nahum 1: 2-3, 6). Citing these Old Testament verses as evidence, I propose that we have a God who has a limit to His patience!

Why is God indignant? Let's try "putting ourselves in His shoes." Suppose you love someone so completely (in God's case, humanity), yet despite your offer of undying love, you are repeatedly rebuffed. If you were the one experiencing this unrequited love, wouldn't you feel the same way God feels? Wouldn't you yearn for that person's love, affection, and fidelity? Wouldn't you suffer the same outrage God expresses in Scripture from being constantly offended, spurned, and ignored? The question then becomes: how much evil is God willing to tolerate in us, the human beings He loves so much?

The Heart of God

To be sure, God wants to change our imperfect hearts if we let Him, for His ultimate desire is that our hearts reflect His own true nature. In fact He promises, "I will give you a new heart...I will take away your stony, stubborn heart and give you a tender, responsive heart" (Ezekiel 36: 25-26). So when we stumble, if we just appeal to God's Generous Heart, we soon discover His graciousness, and we experience His loving-kindness flowing through us, guiding our faltering steps. Here, God's Forbearance is also revealed (Romans 2: 4). This means that no matter how long it takes, the Lord patiently waits for us. It is only when we are willing to love Him, to call upon Him in prayer, that He responds with an outpouring of blessings. Of course, these gifts are *always* contingent upon *our* response to God's love, for He loved us first (1 John 4: 19). When we return this love, we are delighted to honor Him as Almighty Father, another fitting description which denotes the unfathomable greatness of His majesty

(Genesis 17: 1). But also, we honor Him as Savior. This is perhaps His most perfect title. Isaiah 35: 4-7 assures us, "Say to those whose hearts are frightened: Be strong, fear not! Here is your God. He comes with vindication; with divine recompense He comes to save you." In other words, have courage! In fact, the word courage is derived from the Latin word "coeur" which means heart.

We can conclude that honoring the virtuous aspects of God is the key element to a heart-felt relationship with Him. These virtues are the same qualities we admire in Jesus and which He modelled on earth. Fortunately, the Lord makes it easier for us to live in righteousness by promising to augment our efforts. Jeremiah 31: 33 says, "I will put My law within them, and write it in their hearts." This means as we seek to know God's Way, we receive and sustain His Wisdom within us. Likewise, we gain new spiritual insight to discern the right thing to do, for now we have access to God's law written in our hearts. When we achieve this attunement, we can become a "savior" to someone else, someone whom the Lord has put in our path for a purpose. Beyond that, if we could completely comprehend the unfathomable depth of the Heart of God, the immeasurable intensity of His Love for us, we would feel such incredible joy and gratitude that our hearts would naturally overflow! We would want nothing more than to continuously praise, worship, and glorify His Holy Name! Not only that, we would want to share our joy with everyone we meet.

Heart/Mind Connection

As I hinted above, the role of the heart in Scripture reveals a lot more than virtuous qualities, deep emotions and tender feelings. It reveals the importance of Intelligence, this representing another magnificent dimension of the Creator's total Being. In the natural world, we observe and admire this Intelligence which expresses itself as science and mathematics, literature and poetry, music and art. Just as knowledge, understanding, beauty, joy, and harmony are aspects of God's Heart, so too are right thinking and proper action. When all these things combine - when our feeling self (the heart) unites with our thinking self (the mind) - they produce what I call the heart/mind connection. In the life of Mary, the Mother of Jesus, a complete alignment of heart and mind finds its perfect expression. We see how Mary "treasured up all these things, pondering them in her heart" (Luke 2: 19). According to the dictionary, to ponder means,

"To think about (something) carefully, especially before making a decision or reaching a conclusion." Mary's example teaches us the meaning of the heart/mind relationship, to feel as well as to think about the circumstances that are affecting our lives, and to bring these feelings and thoughts to prayer. By doing this, our prayer becomes meaningful because it combines a receptive heart with a reflective mind.

Several Scriptures underscore this heart/mind connection. Hebrews 4: 12-13 explains it this way: "The Word of God is living…able to discern reflections and thoughts of the heart." Psalm 15: 2-5 says, "He who walks blamelessly and does justice, who thinks the truth in his heart…shall never be disturbed." Psalm 90: 12-13 exclaims, "Teach us to number our days aright, that we may gain wisdom of heart." In Luke 8: 15, we read, "When they have heard the Word, they hold it fast with a good and upright heart." Proverbs 21: 2 teaches, "Every way of a man is right in his own eyes; but the Lord ponders the hearts." Finally, Colossians 3: 23 says, "Whatever you do, do it with all your heart." Each of these statements reveals the potency of a humble, sincere heart and mind, whose unified desire is intimacy with God.

Most instructive is a statement made by St. Paul, who tells

us, "Be transformed by the renewing of your mind" (Romans 12: 2). Paul exemplifies how right thinking and conduct are indelibly linked to the Heart of God. Also, we recall Jesus' words which explain the need to think about, that is, evaluate, our actions *before* we attempt to pray: "So if you are offering your gift at the altar and there remember that your brother has something against you, leave your gift there before the altar and go. First be reconciled to your brother, and then come and offer your gift" (Matthew 5: 23). Thus purified by thoughtful reflection and appropriate action, we too, can "offer our gift" in the form of prayer. This is the true convergence of a compassionate heart with mindful behavior, and it marks the beginning of a holistic, integrated, and focused prayer.

Praying from the Heart

In 1 Samuel 16: 7, we hear a familiar passage: "The Lord looks upon the heart." To conform to this understanding, the priest says at the consecration of the divine bread during the Catholic Mass, "Lift up your hearts!" and the congregation responds, "We have lifted them up to the Lord!" Why? Because only the heart can express the depth of our praise and worship. As Christians, we often contemplate the Sacred

Heart of Jesus. Why? Because His Heart burns with such ardent love for everyone! Only His exposed and flaming Heart can begin to capture the intense love and passionate desire Jesus feels for the salvation of souls. As depicted in countless statues and paintings throughout the centuries, Jesus points to His Heart, as if inviting us to participate in this great mystery.

Jesus's Heart is always shown encircled with thorns. This reflects His willingness to sacrifice everything for us. Indeed, "God so loved the world that He gave His only begotten Son..." (John 3: 16). The thorns around His Heart teach us that self-sacrifice is a necessary part of our participation and commitment. And so the same passionate love Jesus has for us becomes our burning desire too! (see "Song of Songs" in Lesson 13, "Gaining Wisdom"). After the Resurrection, when two disciples encounter the risen Lord on the road to Emmaus, what strikes them to the core is the immensity of the incomprehensible Heart of God. And their hearts respond in kind: "They exclaim to one another, 'Did not our hearts burn within us, while He talked with us by the way, and while He opened to us the Scriptures?' (Luke 24: 32).

So how do we pray from the heart? As I have shown, the

first step is to know the true nature of the Divine in all of its aspects (The Heart of God), and the second step is to serve Him by acting in righteousness (Heart/Mind Connection). Then, center yourself in prayer, and the Holy Spirit's action will perfect that prayer. When you are well along this path, you may find your empathy and generosity expanding, your intuition increasing, synchronistic events occurring frequently, and most of all, you will feel a profound joy welling up in your heart.

St. Bernard once remarked, "The more things your trust dares to ask of the Lord, the more you will receive." So too, as the soul watches the manifestations of God's grace unfold, it is in awe of His goodness, and dares to ask for more blessings and favors, all the while responding with praise and adoration. When these feelings are brought back to prayer, a cycle begins in which the more love the soul feels, the more trust it develops, and the more remedies of God's grace occur. The more they occur, the more intense is the soul's love and gratitude, which again are brought back to prayer. This "feedback loop" builds upon itself over time. In this way, we receive both interior and exterior graces. But St. Peter Eymard tells us that, "an interior grace is worth more than a thousand external graces." Therefore, it is only when we receive an interior grace that we experience the fullness of God's love. This is one of the many benefits of "Praying from the Heart."

Practice

All of us are called to an ever-closer walk with the Lord, but in order for this to happen, we must *practice* what we know. As I already said, this *practice* involves "renewing our mind" (Romans 12: 2). We can only do this through disciplined, sustained effort. In short, praying from the heart requires our full attention or *mindfulness*, together with *time and patience*. Sadly, many do not do this. They are content with reciting vocal prayers by rote, and they never seriously attempt to cultivate a deeper form, a more loving form of prayer. "Praying from the Heart" means *feeling* the words you say and *listening* for God's response, having in a sense, a "heart-to-heart" conversation. After some time, this naturally becomes *silent* prayer, flowing directly from my heart to God's, and from His Heart to mine. While the recitation of vocal prayers is good, it is only a basic response to God's love. If one stays there and never tries to advance in prayer, there is danger of stagnation, leading to apathy. This can

84

happen because of the repetitive nature of vocal prayers; after a while, they can simply lose their meaning. Perhaps this is why many prayers go unanswered.

False Pride

A word of warning: To those who are confident of their spiritual progress and who look down on everyone else, Jesus offers a parable. It is found in the Gospel of Luke, Chapter 18: 9-14: "Two men went up to the temple to pray, one a Pharisee and the other a tax collector. The Pharisee stood by himself and prayed: 'God, I thank you that I am not like other people—robbers, evildoers, adulterers —or even like this tax collector. I fast twice a week and give a tenth of all I get.' But the tax collector stood at a distance. He would not even look up to Heaven, but beat his breast and said, 'God, have mercy on me, a sinner.' I tell you that this man, rather than the other, went home justified before God. For all those who exalt themselves will be humbled, and those who humble themselves will be exalted." So let's be aware that, after we have gained a measure of spiritual acumen, we may naturally tend toward a prideful and self-righteous attitude. As Jesus shows us in the parable, false pride can slip by without detection and infiltrate our prayer. The remedy is asking God to create in us a pure heart.

A Pure Heart

The Gospel of Matthew 5-7, records the teachings of Jesus known as the "Sermon on the Mount." Chapter 5 contains wise exhortations which are called the Beatitudes, each phrase starting with the words, "Blessed are..." In verse 8, Jesus teaches: "Blessed are the pure of heart, for they shall see God." Here Jesus shows us that when we strive for purity, we create a greater and greater connection with our Heavenly Father. But what is a pure heart? It is about single-mindedness, which is the realization of the heart/mind connection. The Gospel of James, Chapter 1: 5-8, cautions, "But let him ask in faith, with no doubting, for the one who doubts, is like a wave of the sea that is driven and tossed by the wind. For that person must not suppose that he will receive anything from the Lord; he is a double-minded man, unstable in all his ways." Likewise, Jesus advises, "Let your eye be single, and your whole body will be full of light" (Matthew 6: 22). This means to act with boldness, firmly establishing within ourselves an essential blend of heart and mind, creating a harmonious unit which places us at the very threshold of grace. In the final analysis, "No man can serve two masters," Jesus tells us, "for he will either hate the one and love the other; or else he will hold to the one, and despise the other" (Matthew 6: 24). As applied to our prayer life, this means we will eventually make the choice between following the preferred ways of the world or advancing in the spiritual ways of heart-felt prayer.

Their Hearts Will Grow Cold

Romans 12: 11 addresses the problem of lackluster, unproductive prayer. Here the apostle Paul tells Jesus' followers, "Never be lacking in zeal, but keep your spiritual fervor, serving the Lord." Concerning End-Times biblical prophecy, it seems that at some future date, there will be such a lack of fervent prayer that it will extend world-wide; that is, very few people will offer God sincere prayers from the heart. The Bible warns that this situation will contribute to widespread malaise, and it will eventually lead to a general lack of love. Revelation 2: 4 says, "But I have this against you, that you have abandoned the love you had at first." The Gospel of Matthew 24: 12, predicts, "Because of the increase in lawlessness, the hearts of many will grow cold." But of course, this is not a new problem. As far back as 1570, on the heels of the Protestant Reformation, then Pope and Saint Pius

V uttered this audacious statement, "All the evils of the world are due to lukewarm Catholics."

Referring back to Scripture, a final admonition is given against a global apathy which is said to begin during the End-Times. Revelation 3: 15-17 uses harsh words to describe the situation: "I know your works; you are neither cold nor hot. Would that you were either cold or hot! So, because you are lukewarm, and neither hot nor cold, I will spit you out of my mouth. For you say, I am rich, I have prospered, and I need nothing, not realizing that you are wretched, pitiable, poor, blind, and naked. I counsel you to buy from me gold refined by fire, so that you may be rich..." What is this "gold refined by fire," that we are advised to buy? It is the intense love of God! We must acquire it and make it our own. The message is clear; we can never allow ourselves to grow lukewarm, we must not let the apparent comfort of our life, especially our prayer life, lull us into complacency. Our true purpose as Christians is to set our hearts on fire with the love of God! In short, we must learn what it means to "Pray from the Heart."

LESSON SEVEN

PRACTICE

VIGILANCE

PRACTICE VIGILANCE

" Except the Lord build the house, they labor in vain that build it: except the Lord keep the city, the watchman is awake but in vain."

(Psalm 127: 1)

The Watchmen

Sometimes when I read the Bible, certain words or phrases stand out. Recently, I noticed how the word, "watchmen," was used, and I wondered, "Who are they?" A valid question, since they are referenced so often in Scripture. Another question is, "What is God's purpose in mentioning them?" In doing a bit of research, and I found some interesting possibilities. According to gotquestions.org, here is the basic answer:

> Watchmen in the Bible were guards responsible for protecting towns and military installations from surprise enemy attacks and other potential dangers. Ancient Israelite cities often stationed watchmen on high walls or in watchtowers. Their job was to keep

watch and warn the townspeople of impending threats.

There are many references to watchmen who kept an eye out for physical threats in the Bible: "Now the watchman was standing on the tower in Jezreel, and he saw the company of Jehu as he came and said, 'I see a company.' (2 Kings 9: 17). Watchmen safeguarded fields and vineyards during harvest time (Isaiah 5: 1–2; Matthew 21: 33; also Mark 12: 1) and acted as sentinels who announced the start of a new day (Psalm 130: 6; also Isaiah 21: 11-12).

This definition is fine as far as it goes. However, there is a deeper, spiritual meaning to the watchmen's presence in Scripture. Looking first at the Old Testament, I discovered that God appointed prophets whom He designated as watchmen over the souls of the people. "Son of man, I have made you a watchman for the people of Israel; so hear the word I speak and give the warning from me" (Ezekiel 33: 7; also Hosea 9: 8).

Quoting again from gotanswers.org, we read:

Israel's spiritual watchmen bore a heavy responsibility before the Lord. If a prophet failed to warn others as God had appointed him to do, his own life was in danger, and he would be held accountable for the people's sin: "Son of man, speak to your people and say to them: 'When I bring the sword against a land, and the people of the land choose one of their men and make him their watchman, and he sees the sword coming against the land and blows the trumpet to warn the people, then if anyone hears the trumpet but does not heed the warning and the sword comes and takes their life, their blood will be on their own head since they heard the sound of the trumpet but did not heed the watchman's warning' "

(Ezekiel 33: 2-6).

A watchman who was blind or disobedient to the Lord's words left the people he was called to protect open to danger and suffering (Isaiah 56: 10). Obedience is the only course of action for a true watchman: "But if you do warn the wicked person to turn from their ways and they do not do so, they will die for their sin, though you yourself will be saved" (Ezekiel 33: 9)

In short, a prophet's job as watchman was to guide God's people to live faithfully. His unique role was to be forever vigilant, ready to warn the people of impending danger should they repeatedly disregard the Lord and His commandments. As God's official watchman, a prophet was called to identify wicked people and call them out for their treachery. He was not only to confront these evildoers, he was instructed to announce that God's judgment and destruction were upon them! Unless they immediately turned away from their evil ways and amended their lives, there would be dire consequences, and not just for them, but for generations yet to come.

Reluctant Prophets

Some of the people God assigned to do the job were not eager to hold the position. From the biblical saga of Jonah, we observe a very uncooperative prophet trying to escape when God designates him as watchman. After repeatedly fleeing and having endured several harrowing adventures, Jonah ends up in the belly of a whale for three days, begging for mercy. At that point, the whale "vomited him out on dry land" (Jonah 2: 10). Finally, Jonah acquiesces; he will act as the Lord's chosen watchman for Nineveh. So he goes into "the great city" to warn the people that disaster is about to befall them. In this story, we see the severe consequences God imposes on the wayward prophet, but once Jonah decides to comply with God's Will, he receives mercy and strength to carry out his mission. God's mercy also extends to Nineveh, for when the people hear Jonah's words, they choose to heed the warning. Everyone repents "from his evil way and from the violence that is in his hands" (Jonah 3). Because of Jonah's warning, the city is spared from destruction.

Another unlikely prophet destined to become a watchman for Israel is Amos: "Then Amaziah said to Amos, 'Get out, you seer! Go back to the land of Judah. Earn your bread there and do your prophesying there. Don't prophesy anymore at Bethel, because this is the king's sanctuary and the temple of the kingdom' "(Amos 7: 12-13). Verses 14-15 continue, "Amos answered Amaziah, 'I was neither a prophet nor the son of a prophet, but I was a shepherd, and I also took care of sycamore-fig trees. But the Lord took me from tending the flock and said to me, 'Go, prophesize to my people Israel.' "Although skeptical, Amos obeys God's command. And even though he is met with resistance, he becomes a spiritual watchman for God's people.

Watches of the Night

History tells us that ancient Greeks and Romans, as well as the Jewish people, divided the night into military "watches." When Rome dominated the culture, the Jewish watches were conformed according to Roman reckoning. Thus they added "a fourth watch." These demarcations of time were, "Even," "Midnight," "Cock crowing," and "Morning." The first watch was from sunset to 9 pm, the second from 9 pm to midnight, the third from midnight to 3 am, and the fourth from 3 am until 6 am. There are several biblical references concerning the watches of the night. Sometimes these verses refer to the necessity of waiting. Other times, they equate to a heavenly perspective of time.

The first passage I will mention is from Psalm 130, which speaks of the soul who longingly waits for the Lord, "counting on His Word." Here the watchman is linked to patient endurance, and as the watchman watches and waits, so must we. Therefore, the psalmist's prayer is ours too: "My soul longs for the Lord, more than the watchman for daybreak. Let the watchman count on daybreak, and Israel on the Lord, because with the Lord there is mercy and fullness of redemption" (V 5-7).

The Old Testament Song of Songs, also known as Song of Solomon or Canticle of Canticles, tells a similar story of watchfulness. This book is thought to be an allegory describing the Church as the Bride of Christ, who is searching for her Beloved. The passage below includes a reference to the night watchmen. In this symbolic story, we are shown that a certain amount of time must elapse before the Beloved, who is Jesus Christ, is fully revealed. Here is Song of Songs, from Chapter 3: 1-5:

> At night on my bed,
>
> I looked for the one I love
>
> I looked for him, but I could not find him.
>
> I got up and went around the city,
>
> In the streets and squares
>
> Looking for the one I love
>
> I looked for him, but I could not find him.
>
> The watchmen found me as they patrolled the city
>
> So I asked, "Have you seen the one I love?

As soon as I had left them,

I found the one I love

I held him and would not let him go

Until I brought him to my mother's house,

To the room where I was born.

Finding the Beloved as soon as she left the watchmen, indicates that it is she (who symbolizes the Church) and not the watchmen (secular men) who is alert to and prepared for the Divine encounter. Thus, the Church is presented as tirelessly active and vigilant in her search for her Lord. For more about the Song of Songs, see Lesson 13, "Gaining Wisdom."

The last Old Testament passage I will highlight is from Psalm 90: 4, where the passage of time is seen from an otherworldly view. Here the psalmist declares, "A thousand years in your sight are like a day that has just gone by, or like a watch in the night." This reference to "a watch in the night" is meant to give us some idea of how inscrutable God's heavenly reckoning of time is.

In the New Testament, there are more narratives which speak of the watchmen and the watches of the night.

Matthew 14 explains how Jesus appeared to His disciples, walking on water. When He beckoned the apostle Peter to come to Him, this happened during the fourth watch (V 25). Setting the time must have been important to the story. Perhaps the fact that it was nearly daybreak, the last watch of the night, is significant. Jesus had gone up the mountain and had been praying by Himself all night, leaving the disciples alone in a boat "tossed by the waves." The implication is that He waited until the last possible moment to rescue them. Did Jesus do this in order to test their faith?

Before the crucifixion, Jesus predicted Peter would deny Him three times before the cock crowed. This is a reference to "Cock crowing," or the third watch of the night, from midnight to 3 am (Matthew 26: 75). The precise timing of the Passion events may be viewed symbolically, since the next phase of it was to occur during the fourth and final watch of the night. This is when they tortured Jesus, and prepared Him for His impending death. The fourth watch begins at the darkest hour, the time right before the dawn. Consequently, it heralds the start of "a new day." In this case, it is a day unlike any other in human history, a day which brought with it the crucifixion of Jesus and our redemption. As "a new day," it certainly ushered in a fresh start for humanity, as the beginnings of Christianity took shape on that very morning.

Watchmen for Today

Although not a contemporary saint, I chose Thomas More as an example. This is because he acted as God's appointed watchman during a very turbulent time in religious history. According to Wikipedia:

> More opposed the Protestant Reformation, directing polemics against the theology of Martin Luther, Huldrych Zwingli, John Calvin, and William Tyndale. More also opposed Henry VIII's separation from the Catholic Church, refusing to acknowledge Henry as supreme head of the Church of England and the annulment of his marriage to Catherine of Aragon. After refusing to take the Oath of Supremacy, he was convicted of treason and executed. On his execution, he was reported to have said: "I die the King's good servant, and God's first."

Are there courageous watchmen around us today? In our self-absorbed world, they can be hard to spot, but I identified three contemporary figures whom I think deserve the title:

Martin Luther King, Pope Francis, and Greta Thunberg. In the first instance, Martin Luther King's mission was to vigorously defend his people against racial injustice while promoting civil rights for all. Pope Francis focuses his energies on climate issues and the defense of the poor and marginalized, especially the soaring immigrant populations. Greta Thunberg, a teenage activist who travels the world, rails against the staunch resistance of those in power to address the climate crisis. Among these three "watchmen," Greta is the most vocal, the most assertive in her words and actions. Greta communicates the urgency of the situation like no one else, insisting there is no more time to delay. If we don't implement radical measures quickly, she believes in less than ten years, life on earth will not be sustainable. A newly published state-of-the-science climate report just released by the United Nations confirms her deepest fears. Greta is truly a brave watchman for our modern times.

Two Lessons

By considering the watchmen - those in Scripture, those who lived more recently, as well as the famous personalities of today - we notice there are two important lessons for us. The first concerns the physical world. It is time to "Wake up!

Do what is right and do it now!" The second lesson has both physical and spiritual implications. Our contemporary watchmen warn, "Be ever vigilant, alert, and prepared, for sooner or later, you will have to face the consequences of decades of wrongdoing by both self and others."

As it was in ancient times, so it is today; the watchmen deliver fearful and threatening messages. They remind us of our apathy and inaction. They tell us that we must not allow the complacency and greed of the world to paralyze us. We must act, doing whatever is within our power to defend what is right. In our times, this involves political, humanitarian, and environmental action. If we act, the Lord Himself promises a remedy for a seemingly hopeless situation. This is verified by King Solomon whose wisdom exhorts us to "keep watch at the gate," that is, always stay attentive to the Word of God. Only then will there be resolution. As we engage in the struggle, the Lord provides a safe harbor from the storms raging around us (Proverbs 8: 34-35). Perhaps we experience this safety and security in our lifetime, but if not, we will definitely experience it in the next (V 36). The degree of success we attain here on earth will not determine the reward we receive in Heaven. It is only the sincere *effort* we put forth to affect change that will count in the end.

The watchmen's warnings are clear; we must maintain constant vigilance and we must take action against all wrongdoing. Matthew 24: 42-44 sums it up this way: "Therefore keep watch, because you do not know the day on which your Lord will come. But understand this, if the homeowner had known in which watch of the night the thief was coming, he would have kept watch and would not have let his house be broken into. For this reason, you also must be ready, because the Son of Man will come at an hour you do not expect."

LESSON EIGHT

THE NEED FOR

OBEDIENCE

THE NEED FOR

OBEDIENCE

" If a man is just and does what is right...

he has withdrawn his hand from evildoing."

(Ezekiel 18: 5-8)

The Great Deceiver

For Christians, it's a no-brainer. We all know who the great deceiver is, none other than Lucifer, the devil himself, "the father of lies" (John 8: 44). And of course, we know the biblical story where it all began - in the Garden of Eden. Eve was tricked by the devil who, disguised as a serpent, enticed her into eating the fruit from the Tree of the Knowledge of Good and Evil (Genesis 3). I wonder if the devil worked on Eve for quite a while before she finally gave in to his temptation. Eve knew because God had told her, "If you eat of the fruit from that tree, or even touch it, you will die" (V 3). Indeed, this may be an allegorical, rather than a literal story, but the essential revelation is the same; a disruptive and wicked force exists in our world which tries to separate us from the love of a benevolent Creator.

For the moment, let's take a literal approach. From this perspective, did you ever wonder why the devil would bother to tempt Eve in the first place? What exactly was in it for him? Did he know that tricking her would literally have eternal consequences? Perhaps his motive was revenge. Disobedience to God had pushed him out of heaven, and he was determined to get even. Or, if he could get just one person to disobey God, would the rest of humanity follow suit? Apparently, his bet paid off. Adam too, ate the forbidden fruit.

Then there is the question of pride. Being prideful is the opposite of obedience because a certain amount of humility must be present in order to override the ego and do what another wants - in other words, to obey. In the devil's case, his pride is not just that he refuses to do this. He aspires to be like God, that is, all powerful; he wants to BE God! Such ego-centrism declares, "I will NOT obey!" This one, brazen announcement set the stage for the perennial story which we know all too well. It is the classic, archetypal saga of the on-going battle between good and evil, and it continues to unfold and reverberate throughout history to the present day. Lesson 5, "Choose Life," discusses this topic.

Abraham

The biblical narrative of Abraham, who is esteemed as the father of the Jewish people, as well as the father of Islam and Christianity, demonstrates the importance of obedience. In Genesis 22 we find the story of the testing of Abraham. Facing what must have been agonizing uncertainty, and in denying his own natural inclinations, Abraham remains faithful; He trusts God and obeys. Verse 21 in James 2 remarks, "Was not our father Abraham considered righteous for what he did when he offered his son Isaac on the altar?" At the end of the story, Abraham's obedience to God is richly rewarded. This is because, "In hope against hope he believed, so that he might become a father of many nations according to that which had been spoken" (Romans 4: 18). The biblical account of Abraham embodies the archetypal theme of the hero who must suffer long, painful trials, all of which lead to the successful completion of his mission, and finally, to an incredibly abundant life. In some versions of this classic story, the hero dies at the end, as Moses did before reaching the Promised Land (Numbers 20: 12; also Deuteronomy 34:

4-5). But it was by God's design that Abraham lived and prospered, as did Job, another heroic figure found in Scripture (Job 42: 10-17). Both Abraham and Job were recompensed "a hundred-fold" for their perseverance, fidelity, and total obedience.

Today Lies Proliferate

We live in an age where huge amounts of disinformation abound, unparalleled in human experience. Yet, it is also true that the range and consequences of propaganda with its deliberate falsehoods are nothing new. You don't have to look far back in history to recall Hitler's lies against the Jews, or to identify the far right political roots which led to the rapid rise of Fascism ("On Tyranny: 20 Lessons from the 20th Century," by Timothy Snyder, 2017). More recently, in 1994 in Rwanda, hatred and violence were advocated against a minority group of the country's own people, through repetitious radio broadcasts, the preferred social media of the day. An endless barrage of vicious verbal attacks spewed forth from that platform, resulting in a mass genocide where millions of innocent people died. This debacle was predicted and could have been prevented, as you will see in Lesson 17, "End-Times Prophecy."

Unlike in former times, today we contend with the immense influence of mass media. It has revolutionized the way most of the world receives, and gets its understanding of current events. What people ingest through media, becomes their "truth." Yet, so much outright deception is circulating that the negative effects of it are burgeoning into every area of life. We now have unprecedented levels of drug and sex trafficking, the proliferation of weapons and gun violence, deep hatred against certain minority and ethnic groups, and the establishment of extreme vigilante and militia factions. Sadly, social media platforms have also brought countless, vulnerable youth to the brink of suicide. But the explosion of mass media is not to blame. It is only one of many instruments the devil uses to confuse us, and to turn us away from what is right and just. As we try to negotiate the rough terrain of our lives in these turbulent conditions, the devil's tactics become more aggressive against civil law and the moral code.

What does the proliferation of lies have to do with obedience? When we realize the extent of damage the devil has wrought, we witness the fact that his cunning strategies work! He has manipulated humanity to disobey God by bombarding it with deceptions, parading an endless stream of false gods and false ideologies before us. With lightning speed, these fraudulent or enticing prospects are presented until we can no longer resist their shallow appeal. The reality is the devil will attack from every possible angle, usually in the areas where we are most vulnerable. He attempts to beat us into submission by employing his very own brand of seductive reasoning. And the devil is absolutely thrilled when we act upon his alluring proposals. He loathes our loyalty and obedience to God, and he will do everything he can to thwart it.

Recognizing Falsehood

The psalmist prays, "Hear, O Holy Lord, and consider my supplication; give ear to my prayer that proceeds not from deceitful lips" (Psalm 16: 1). If we ourselves utter falsehoods, we cannot hope to receive an answer to prayer. Moreover, we cannot be obedient to God.

You might say that recognizing falsehood is the key to obedience. But as you will see in the next Lesson, "Finding Truth," people are so accustomed to lies that they no longer are able to recognize them as false. Not only that, they spread what they have heard, thinking they are performing a service, while actually they are promoting disorder and mayhem. Today, lies and lying have polarized people to the point where they quickly reject any "truth" that does not conveniently match their own viewpoint. Try talking sense or logic to these people, and you will soon find out it is futile. The rational mind, once revered and respected as "scientific," is now met with utmost suspicion and scorn. Conspiracy theories abound. What was once true at face value, is countered by skepticism and denial.

We are currently witnessing, "Cultural Totalitarianism." An Italian Philosopher named Augusto Del Noce coined this phrase to describe the phenomenon of the ascendency of politics over culture. Politics has once again become the undisputed, driving force that dictates social values. To the degree that it does so, it constitutes a dangerous and unholy situation. As indicated by students of world history, we are again approaching the same slippery slope of lies and propaganda that mankind has gone down before ("On Tyranny: 20 Lessons from the 20th Century," by Timothy Snyder, 2017).

So how can we obey God in such irrational circumstances?

If we are ever to perceive what He is calling us to do, our only recourse is to ask for His intervention in our lives. That way, we will begin to understand what true obedience to Him really means for us today.

Obedience and COVID-19

Let's examine events of the past two years, 2020 and 2021. I will offer a small illustration of how false claims, disinformation, and distrust have led to widespread disobedience. I am not talking about the civil disobedience of Henry David Thoreau, who advocated non-violent resistance against slavery. Rather, this is a deliberate, mindless disregard for the health and safety of others in the name of one's personal freedom. After all, the devil wants you to think that you are all-important. In fact, you alone matter; you are above the law, you are equal to God!

In the beginning of 2020, before the COVID-19 pandemic began, people were generally active, happy, and business was good. We obviously prefer this comfortable lifestyle since it gives us freedom to pursue our goals and to meet and socialize with others. But when this open lifestyle began to fade, many people clung to what they wanted instead of embracing the small sacrifices that were required of them at the time. As COVID-19 spread and turned into a national and global pandemic, these same people refused to accept its severity. They thought the threat to health and safety was totally overblown, or that there was some sort of conspiracy going on.

In the end, obedience means taking personal responsibility. I believe the contemptuous disregard of the precautionary measures put in place when COVID-19 arrived at our doorstep, was just another form of the devil's proud and defiant declaration, "I will NOT obey!" He abhors responsible behavior. During the first wave of the pandemic, he encouraged you to assert your rights: He told you that if you don't want to, you don't have to quarantine, or wear face masks, social distance, or the like. You must defend your freedom! So you should feel free to party, or do whatever else you want with impunity. To me, this attitude is a flagrant display of disobedience.

Have We Learned Anything?

Since that time, one short-term effect of non-compliance has been "super-spreader events" which have contributed to a rapid resurgence of the virus. Moreover, in the past three months, COVID-19 has reappeared in a new, mutated, and more virulent form known as the Delta variant. This "virus-turned-mutant" is poised to usher in a spectacular revival of the disease. Nevertheless, today's headlines report there are thousands of people protesting in major cities throughout the world against the very real prospect that regulations such as mask-wearing in all public places and perhaps even lockdowns may be imposed again. Of course, the protestors demand that everything remain open with absolutely no restrictions. Their signs read, "No More Mandates!" Indeed, they are in no mood to tolerate the imposition of any new rules which will curtail their free expression. The problem is cases are rising so rapidly in our country that local and state governments may have no other choice. The disease is regaining momentum in other parts of the world as well, including Japan, where the Olympic Games have begun. Despite the ubiquitous spread of the deadly Delta variant, there is too much financially at stake to close down the event. Fortunately, many precautions have been taken, but I guess it was inevitable that some athletes would get sick. This is an unfortunate situation indeed.

To get informed about the subject of pandemics, you can read an excellent account of the many regional and global episodes that have occurred throughout human history. You will discover that these kinds of health crises are not new, having happened many times before, including in modern times. It was only the swift action of some courageous scientists that narrowly averted a world-wide outbreak not once, but several times in recent history. ("The Coming Plague: Newly Emerging Diseases in a World Out of Balance," by Laurie Garrett, 1994).

Trusting the Science

A vaccine roll-out that started strong, has recently fizzled. Some folks still "don't believe the science," or state flatly that the vaccine is unapproved, and therefore suspect. What they fail to see is that the drugs used to save the lives of thousands suffering from COVID-19 are also unapproved, yet thankfully, they work. Without emergency approval for these special drugs, who knows how many additional patients would have died? Currently, infection rates are on the rise again in most states, but this time at least, it appears some hold-outs against the vaccine are starting to relent. A lot more people have decided to get vaccinated than was true just a few short months ago. This is a hopeful sign.

In hindsight, experts conclude that if a larger percentage of people had gotten vaccinated much sooner, at the onset of the pandemic, COVID-19 would not have had the chance to mutate and gain such virulence. I believe them, but there are still vast numbers of people who don't. Some simply refuse the vaccine because they decided long ago to step aside. Despite the alarming resurgence of the disease, they prefer to maintain their original "Wait and See" attitude. Also, there is a large number of African American communities who strongly resist the vaccine. This is because in the past, they have been deceived by the medical profession and they harbor a deeply rooted, justifiable distrust. One such debacle which gained notoriety recently is the Tuskegee Experiment of 1932. Because of the fallout created by that demeaning episode, strongly held objections against the medical establishment and its sometimes-dubious methodologies remain. Lastly, among those who steadfastly refuse to get vaccinated are those who won't let go of their pet conspiracy theory and with it, an array of false "facts." Among this number are ultra-conservative Christians who unwittingly spread the lie that the vaccines were produced by some Big

Brother-type, demonic entity which has laced them with toxins, and whose sinister plot is to use them as a means for global control, thus ushering in the final days of the biblical Book of Revelation. Taking the vaccine is for them, accepting the dreaded "Mark of the Beast." (Revelation 13-14).

Because of these factors, the United States may fail to achieve herd immunity with about 70% of the country's population receiving the required two doses, and now possibly a third one. At the same time, we are already seeing "breakthrough" infections, and this doesn't bode well for the future. Yet despite the odds, all evidence points to the evolution of vaccine science as our best hope for getting ahead of a virus that continues to mutate. Nevertheless, if enough people remain stubborn and unwilling to follow science in this regard, the scenario we started with in the beginning of the pandemic may have to play out again, not just one more time, but several. Let's hope not.

Why is it we never hear people say, "Trust God," but we often hear people advising us to, "Trust the science"? In the end, trusting God must come first. As I've explained, there is sound reasoning behind advocating science. For all its deficits, it is still the only option we have to find a cure for disease. Yet without God, science alone can never suffice. Luckily, many research scientists are Catholic and many more are practicing Christians. This is an unknown fact, and perhaps their faith is the reason why we are not in even deeper trouble than we are in already.

Obedience in Scripture

I want to get back to the subject of obedience as revealed in Scripture. What Jesus says and does concerning obedience to lawful authority may surprise you. The first event I will highlight occurs when the Pharisees decide to trap Jesus. They approach Him, asking, "Is it lawful to pay taxes?" If He says yes, the people will turn against Him because they resented having to obey a foreign power (the Roman occupation). Besides, the taxes were unjust, and they unfairly burdened the people. If Jesus says no to the question the Pharisees pose, the Roman officials will likely arrest Him for advocating tax evasion! Jesus answers instead by saying, "Render to Caesar what is Caesar's, and to God what is God's." By this, Jesus instructs us to follow the civil law, even if we disagree with it. But we are also bound to follow God's law (Matthew 22: 15– 22). Evidently, the questioners are impressed with Jesus' reply. Verse 22 says that "when they heard it, they marveled. Unable to trap him any further and satisfied with the answer, they went away."

A second story illustrates the same point. Here the apostle Peter needs money to pay for the temple tax, and he went to Jesus asking what to do. After conceding that they are "free persons" and not subject to the tax, Jesus nevertheless tells Peter, "So as not to offend them, go to the sea, throw out a hook, and the first fish which comes up, open its mouth and you will find a coin; take it and give it for me and for you." (Matthew 17: 24-27). Thus, Jesus confirms our obligation to do as the law prescribes.

In Romans 13: 6-7, there is a third example of what our attitude should be when asked to follow legitimate authority. It says, "This is also why you pay taxes: Rulers are working for God and give their time to their work. Pay everyone what you owe them: taxes to those you owe taxes, fees to those you owe fees, respect to those you owe respect, and honor to those you owe honor."

The ultimate act of obedience is Jesus's willingness to suffer and die on the cross for us. Many times, He told His disciples that He came to earth in order to do the Will of the

Father. Hebrews 8: 5 tells us, "He learned obedience from the things He suffered."

Obedience and Humility

Whether the topic is politics, COVID-19, or science, it comes down to the same thing. In all cases, obedience means turning away from lies and wrongdoing, from all unethical and immoral behavior. Of necessity, obedience requires the relentless pursuit of goodness inspired by humility. We choose to abide by Jesus' teachings because His Words lead us to total freedom in righteousness (John 8: 36).

But as we become more mature in our thinking, we realize it is not enough to obey the legal and moral mandates set forth for us. We must also be willing to serve others. "Whosoever wants to become great among you, must be your servant" (Matthew 20: 20-28). This servitude is a true expression of humility, and it becomes the natural role of a person who follows the Lord and is obedient to Him.

In these essays, I often reference the Jesuit priest, Fr. Walter Ciszek. You may recall that his book, "He Leadeth Me," relates the story of his years of imprisonment in solitary confinement, and later in the Siberian labor camps during

World War II. As you might expect, Fr. Ciszek had a lot of time to reflect upon his horrific plight, but he always found the grace to see God's hand at work throughout his excruciatingly painful ordeal.

There are many gems of wisdom in his book, but one to recount here is Fr. Ciszek's understanding of Perfect Obedience as exemplified by Jesus' words to the Heavenly Father, "Thy Will be done." The author reminds us that these words were "uttered in the garden...just before the hours of His greatest trials and humiliations." According to Fr. Ciszek, they signify not so much Jesus' obedience to the Father, but "they are in fact the most perfect illustration of the virtue of humility." He elaborates on this theme, explaining how perfect obedience is always preceded by perfect humility. Ultimately, the author concludes that these two virtues, humility followed by obedience, are really one and the same thing ("He Leadeth Me," by Fr. Walter J. Ciszek, S.J., 1973).

Exceptions to the Rule

The line in the sand that used to mark a clear distinction between lawful and unlawful activity, has blurred. Because of this, I must point out two, glaring exceptions concerning obedience to legitimate authority: abortion and excessive police violence. Both of these things must be considered exclusions from what I said earlier in this essay about obedience. Such issues are good examples of where discretion is needed. In the case of abortion, we can never accept it, but by our active dissent, we are not disobeying civil law.

Regarding police brutality, it is clear that their inexcusable and aggressive conduct is neither lawful nor justified. Therefore, we must not support such actions. Here I am talking about the use of excessive force against defenseless people, coupled with a blatant disregard for human life and dignity on the part of an increasingly militarized police. Although we must still show law enforcement due respect, the depraved behavior of some "bad actors" has denied police everywhere the honor of being our unquestionable, "lawful authority." An appropriate response to the incivility perpetrated by certain segments of the police force, is vehement but peaceful protest.

Who or What is Lawful Authority?

In these trying times, you might ask, "Who or what should I obey?" I admit it is easy to be fooled or to fool ourselves into believing that some rules just don't apply to us. That's why so many of the most popular attitudes and opinions of our day are not based on truth, but on selfishness. Therefore, they circumvent the entire question of obedience. In a period of high tension and emotional distress when so many people are hurting, it is easy to see how this can happen, and how we can fall into an irrational state of not knowing who to trust. And it is also clear how tempting (I use this word intentionally) it is for all of us to find fault with, disregard, or discredit those who are in lawful positions of authority.

That being said, dark clouds are looming on the horizon regarding all civil authority, in the United States as well as abroad. Here in this country, we are in the midst of an epic struggle to maintain our fragile democracy and to hold on to the basic rights we hold dear. In other countries of the world, people are fighting against oppressive authoritarian regimes. It seems that everywhere there are new, escalating and intensifying developments which occur almost daily, constantly shifting the global axis of power. We are truly in unstable and rebellious times. The next Lesson, "Finding Truth," reveals how the erosion of our most cherished values and institutions has led the United States into accepting a new and frightful definition of what "lawful authority" means. This counterfeit "authority" runs amuck of true justice and has entirely lost its moral compass. It is a trend which should deeply concern us.

As I've said, fault-finding and the misrepresentation of facts are the devil's primary game and he is excellent at it. He will try to thoroughly confuse you to the point where you can no longer discern between right and wrong, between God's will for you and your own aberrant judgement. As Fr. Ciszek advises, the best defense is always found in prayer coupled with a true spirit of humility. In the long run, this is what obedience consists of: taking the time to find out what is required of us, confirming it in prayer, and then doing it to the best of our ability. This is the Obedience that God desires from us all.

LESSON NINE

FINDING

TRUTH

FINDING TRUTH

" None call for justice, nor any pleads for truth:
they trust in vanity, and speak lies; they conceive
mischief, and bring forth iniquity."

(Isaiah 59: 4)

What is Truth?

J esus expects us to address the perplexing dilemma of, "What is truth?" just as Pontius Pilate demanded a response from Him about this very question. It seems to me that today's political climate is similar to what Jesus experienced when He was on earth. But in recent memory, there has been no other time where the flagrant disregard and disrespect for facts and for moral integrity have been so widespread.

It reminds me of what the Bible has to say about the End-Times: "But mark this: There will be terrible times in the last days. People will be lovers of themselves, lovers of money, boastful, proud, abusive, disobedient to their parents, ungrateful, unholy, without love, unforgiving, slanderous, with-out self-control, brutal, not lovers of the good, treacherous, rash, conceited, lovers of pleasure rather than lovers of God" (2 Timothy 3: 1-4). Over a decade ago, Mother Teresa of Calcutta already saw this trend unfolding, and she made the comment: "In the developed countries there is a lack of intimacy, a poverty of spirit, of loneliness, of lack of love. There is no greater sickness in the world than that one" ("My Life with the Saints" by James Martin, S.J. 2006).

Returning again to the biblical passages above, St. Paul warns about those who engage in and perpetuate blatant and insidious corruption. He tells his disciple Timothy to "have nothing to do with such people," for they are, "ever learning, and never able to come to the knowledge of the truth" (2 Timothy 3: 7). In the next chapter, Paul restates the message, saying, "They will turn their ears away from the truth and turn aside to falsehood" (2 Timothy 4: 4). These admonitions seem very pertinent for our turbulent times, since they appear to reflect the exact state of affairs we are in today. If Paul's words were meant to be prophetic for the present era, then we must heed them as the final warnings. For more on this topic, see Lesson 17," End-Times Prophecy."

Political Turmoil

In recent years, the issue of truth-telling became a hot topic. Back in December, 2017, the New York Times felt obligated to publish an article entitled, "Trump's Lies." Here is the first paragraph from that article:

> Many Americans have become accustomed to President Trump's lies. But as regular as they have become, the country should not allow itself to become numb to them. So we have catalogued nearly every outright lie he has told publicly since taking the oath of office. Updated: The President is still lying, so we've added to this list, taking it through Nov. 11, and we provided links to the facts in each case.

What legacy was left behind by the last administration? Nothing less than societal discord and distrust. The widespread acceptance of fraudulent claims, despite the antagonism it causes, has birthed a new social norm which encourages and condones lies. Having become "normal" in our culture, these things are now woven into the very fabric of American life. With disinformation rampant today, it is getting harder and harder to discern what is really true and factual. Many have become cold-hearted and stubborn about this, routinely ignoring even objective information such as video documentation, refusing to accept what is right before their very eyes.

The most notable "Big Lie" of our time is that Trump actually won the 2020 presidential election. The strategy is to get as many people to believe this lie as possible. Republicans learned well from the Trump playbook: if you repeat something often enough, some segment of the public will begin to accept it as truth, even if it is not true. And they will act upon it, as we saw on January 6, 2021, when our nation's Capital was attacked. Four hallmarks of demonic activity were on display that day: chaos, violence, destruction, and murder.

Despite such deplorable behavior, the election results continue to be challenged, with the challengers refusing to accept that Biden won a legitimate, free, and fair election. As I write this, a growing number of states are conducting third party audits, pouring over election results hoping to find some evidence of fraud. The legality of allowing the recount of votes by unauthorized entities, votes which had been officially validated and certified, is questionable at best. If these and other perversions are allowed to stand, the devil will have succeeded in snatching our core American values away from us, turning more of us into cold, heartless, and vengeful people. We will then find ourselves estranged from a loving God.

In Congress, ultra-conservatives proudly flaunt their arrogance by refusing to cooperate with moderates, no matter what the issue is. Legislative stalemates occur because partisan politics provides the only motivation to do anything. According to the Gun Violence Archive, an average of ten mass shootings have occurred *every week* in the United States so far this year, as we reach August 2021. Public Television recently reported that in just the past month alone, 1.8 million guns were sold in this country! As outrageous as these statistics are, Congress will not pass the smallest bit of gun control legislation. Meanwhile, gun rights activists clamor about defending their personal right to bear arms, as if the 2nd Amendment of our Constitution would magically disappear if some basic, common-sense changes in the gun laws were made. The truth is most of our legislators are too timid to act; they fear retribution from both party officials and their right-wing constituency.

When it comes to the economy and the middle class, it is a similar story, for here too, there is a great divide in opinion. Of course, the rift has been exacerbated by COVID-19, but the seeds of division were planted before the pandemic arrived. The argument put forth by fiscal conservatives is that the huge tax breaks given to wealthy corporations and the generous tax advantages given to the rich by the past administration, benefited most Americans. The fact is, they didn't. We are told that those financial perks have a "trickle-down effect," that eventually, they profit the middle class. Sadly, they don't. Not only that, but these same tax breaks also contributed Two Trillion dollars to the US deficit, this according to Biden's Presidential Address to Congress on April 28, 2021. The most current statistics substantiate this claim, and they also show the rich are still getting richer, and the poor are still getting poorer. Only now, the gap is even wider than it has ever been before (Pew Research: "Trends in U.S. Income and Wealth Inequality," January 2020).

As if these sorry tales were not enough, the headlines in today's news speak about politically motivated attempts to undermine the very foundations of our democracy! Sinister forces are at work to curtail voting rights and to deny peaceful protesters the right to assemble. Even more egregious is the fact that certain states are actually proposing laws which would make it legal to run over protesters with your car, effectively using it as a deadly weapon!

The latest affront to truth comes from Ireland. Churches in the Irish Republic have been closed since Christmas, 2020, because of the COVID-19 pandemic. As I write this, the Irish government decided to use the virus as an excuse to pass a new law, making it a criminal offense to attend Mass, in fact, banning all public worship indefinitely! According to the Hawaii Catholic Herald, April 30, 2021, the new law "was introduced in a clandestine manner and without notice or consultation." The original report comes from the Catholic News Service. Thankfully, that article concludes, "Similar bans – including in Scotland – have been found to be unlawful." But this is a wake-up call for all of us, because we have seen how brazen the devil has become; he will do anything in his power to turn us away from God.

Recently, I perceived a glimmer of light on the political horizon. The Infrastructure Bill passed both House and Senate yesterday with bipartisan support. This achievement reminds us that instead of giving way to cynicism, we can remain cautiously optimistic; in spite of appearances to the contrary, people in positions of authority are still able to work together for the common good.

Bullying

In order to better understand the biblical view of truth, I chose Revelation 14: 4-5, because it connects truth with goodness: "And in their mouth was found no deceit; for they were without fault." Therefore, what the mouth speaks is important. Words are powerful and have consequences. Jesus tells us this in Matthew 15: 11: "What goes into someone's mouth does not defile them, but what comes out of their mouth, that is what defiles them." And in Mathew 5:20, Jesus warns, "Whosoever shall say, 'Thou fool' shall be in danger of the hell of fire." Yet today, disrespectful or "snarky" comments seem to be the norm, especially on the internet. Using derogatory language is not truth-telling, it is slander. No surprise that cyber-bullying, school bullying, and teen suicides are all on the rise.

In the harsh reality of contemporary life, blatant racism and the use of racial slurs are one more indicator of how far from civil our society has become. It starts with intolerance of others, as well as ongoing tolerance for demeaning, obscene, and vulgar language, especially inside social media. Such behavior fosters a toxic environment that lowers the bar for what is socially acceptable. Lowering the bar means you can say anything you want and get away with it. This trend portends a steady moral decline, and accepting such behavior moves us farther away from the truth.

Truth Equals Compassion

Romans 10:12 says, "For there is no distinction between Jew and Greek; for the same Lord is Lord of all, abounding in riches for all who call on Him." Yet as a nation, we continue to mistreat anyone who is different from us, and so racial tensions continue to mount. Black Americans face horrendous, on-going injustices, while anti-Asian and anti-Semitic assaults are making headlines. It is our shame as Americans that such hate is allowed to fester in our culture. The truth is, we must proclaim and defend our status as brothers and sisters, made by the same loving Creator. We must treat everyone as we would treat Jesus Himself. "Verily I say unto you, inasmuch as you have done it unto one of the least of these my brethren, you have done it unto Me" (Matthew 25: 40-45).

St. John tells us, "He that says I know Him, and does not keep His commandments is a liar and the truth is not in him" (1 John 2: 3-4). In other words, if we really want to know God and His Truth, we must obey His teachings. Otherwise, we are just deceiving ourselves and others. Likewise, we cannot deny Jesus' mandate to extend our love and compassion to the poor and afflicted. He is the Good Shepherd who goes out of His way to rescue the countless numbers of lost, oppressed, marginalized, and outcast people of the world (John 10: 14-15). This is a good place to admit Jesus includes refugees in this group. And certainly, the vast majority of refugees seeking asylum are not "criminals and drug dealers." Always remember that the Holy Family – Mary, Joseph, and the infant Jesus - were political refugees themselves, fleeing to Egypt in the dead of night to escape the tyranny of Herod and the massacre of the Innocents (Matthew 2: 13-18). Thus, it makes sense for Christians to give aid and loving compassion to those who are fleeing persecution, violence and all forms of abuse, drug cartels, discrimination, and abject poverty.

The Ultimate Deception?

The topic of NDEs (Near Death Experiences) is a subject

that touches upon a deeper, very personal side of truth. When these events were first reported and documented, it was thought that only pleasurable NDE experiences occurred immediately after death, since virtually all those who were resuscitated, who came back to life, proclaimed a blissful heaven where there is no judgement, no guilt, and no hell. If the individuals met a benign being or a "spirit guide" in the afterlife, that entity led them to a beautiful, even exhilarating landscape. I wondered about this: if everyone has a blissful experience after death, then these reports present a real problem for Christians. They go against everything he or she knows by faith to be true.

In his book, "Hell and Back," published in 1993, Dr. Maurice Rawlings, M.D. discusses this topic. Contrary to the prevailing view, he saw more than a few, very scary NDEs in his medical practice. Dr. Rawlings began to document these events. He then questioned why NDE researchers hardly ever mentioned such episodes. He was told it was because these hellish experiences were so rare that they were not worth recording.

Upon closer investigation and after years of research, Dr. Rawlings commented that things had begun to change. More and more people were stepping forward to recount what could only be described as horrible NDE experiences. Out of fear or guilt, such persons had previously chosen not to reveal their frightening experiences in the afterlife. This makes sense; if everyone else has had a joy filled NDE, you would look pretty sad in comparison describing the opposite experience! Since the first reports came out, researchers have learned that for as many as "one in five people who have an NDE, the memory may be traumatic," this according to Nancy Evans Bush in her book, "The Buddha in Hell and Other Alarms," 2016. She states that as far back as 1982, "An extensive Gallup survey showed 28% of the reported NDEs were perhaps unpleasant." Apparently, this study was not widely recognized or accepted at the time. In retrospect, the prevailing view among researchers now is that almost all of the prior reports had been skewed in favor of only pleasurable NDE experiences.

But there remains the prickly question of why had so many "bad actors" experienced exceptionally favorable, "no judgement" NDEs? Dr. Rawlings puts forth a rather shocking theory. According to him, at least some of these pleasurable NDEs were counterfeit. That is to say, the devil, masquerading as a being of light, tricked the person into thinking there were no consequences to his earthly actions. The reason for creating this deception is simple: when the person returned to life, as apparently the devil knew he or she would, that person would go out and promote the false doctrine that you can do whatever you want on earth. Hell simply does not exist. Dr. Rawlings could come up with no other plausible explanation to account for this confounding dilemma.

So what is the truth? It will be interesting to see how ongoing NDE research plays out in the future and what it truly reveals, if anything, about life after death. My opinion is that Hell (and Heaven) do exist. Those who decide in their hearts to reject truth, to do evil, to harbor bitterness or seek revenge, who choose hate over love, or who idolize anything other than the one, true God, cannot enter the Kingdom of Heaven: "Nothing evil will be allowed to enter, nor anyone who practices shameful idolatry and dishonesty—but only those whose names are written in the Lamb's Book of Life" (Revelations 21: 27).

The Love of Truth

In the end we must ask, what does know, and loving truth really mean? Jesuses famously proclaims, "If you abide in My Word, you are truly My disciples, and you will know the truth, and the truth will set you free" (John 8: 31-32). Here Jesus equates 1) living in His loving presence, and 2) following His instructions, with 3) knowing the truth, and 4) living in the freedom of a child of God.

Practically, what does this look like? From what kinds of experiences are we set free? As I have said elsewhere, abiding in the Word, in the love of God, means we are set free from prejudice and criticism; that is, we will not pass judgement on another person: "Judge not that you be not judged. For with the judgment, you pronounce you will be judged, and with the measure you use, it will be measured to you" (Matthew 7: 1-2).

When we stop judging others, it does not mean we condone wrongful behavior. It does not mean we do not call out falsehood when we see it. In other words, we can "judge" a behavior as wrong and try to correct it, without ever "passing judgement" on the person doing it. This concept demands a sensitive heart and profound understanding. And it always requires us to forgive the one who perpetrates the transgression. By doing so, we are set free from resentment, revenge, jealousy, and pride. If we could practice Jesus' teachings perfectly, we would no longer feel trapped by addiction or gluttony, greed or lust. Furthermore, we would not feel the need to be right about everything, nor would we have to know with certainty the next step our life's journey will take. In this way, the truth sets us free from worry, as we ask Jesus to decide the correct course of action for our lives. You can read more about this topic in Lesson 11, "Never Lose Hope."

Where there is no truth, there can only be oppression, divisiveness, disorder, civil unrest, and strife. Remember, these things foment feelings of bitterness and hatred in society, and therefore they are not of the truth; they originate in unrighteousness (James 3: 16). This is why Jesus prayed for unity. It is as if He looked into the future and saw our contemporary world. In His "Prayer for Unity," Jesus entreats the Father, asking that we be one as He and the Father are one (John 17: 20-23). Today's social and political climate is why we need prayers for unity more than ever.

Unless we can find common ground and rediscover our mutual goals, we will be unable to resolve the pressing problems of our time.

Scams

What if we trust people too easily, if we assume the good intentions of others when in fact, they are lying to us? In the case of Scammers, their genius resides in their ability to construct and conceal a carefully crafted snare. The Bible cautions, "Be sober, be vigilant, because your adversary the devil walks about as a roaring lion, seeking whom he may devour" (1 Peter 5: 8). This warning of old can be paraphrased and summed up as follows: "The devil searches the internet and uses all electronic devices, seeking whomever he may destroy." This is not simply hyperbole; it is literally true. Scams can happen through a single phone call, or they can develop over time as the end result of a long, seemingly innocent, correspondence. Either way, the devil's cunning is very efficacious; he will weave a clever story so convincing that you may doubt your own sanity. Sometimes, he conjures up distressful images by which to play upon your sympathies. Other times, he will use your imagination to create enticing daydreams for you to entertain in your mind.

140

With beguiling words, he will try to feed your vanity and your sense of importance. The devil is exceedingly patient too; he will bide his time, waiting for the opportune moment to strike. Often, he will lay low for months, waiting and anticipating his move, all the while cloaked in a veil of stealth and secrecy that is almost impossible to penetrate. Then one day he suddenly attacks.

Cruel and heartless, the perpetrator who works the scam is truly under demonic control. Usually, he acts as an impersonator, having stolen someone else's identity. Once you are duped, he may request your private information, such as your social security number, or he may demand a sum of money. It will be just a small amount at first, so no harm done, right? Unfortunately, if you give in, he will soon require more, and it just escalates from there. You are stunned and helpless; you are caught in a trap! To avoid this all-too-common scenario, always be on guard against such things. Pay attention to "red flags," the early warning signs that something is amiss. Since we are human, you may spot warning signs that aren't really there, while you may miss warning signs that really are there. But it is better to err on the side of caution. Without a doubt, the subterfuge I am describing is despicable, and it is always demonic in origin. Only a few short years ago, no one would have suspected such treachery would flourish and propagate at the alarming rates it has today. And at the same time, this diabolical activity remains cleverly masked, luring in the shadows, and for the most part, it stays hidden and undetectable.

Is Science the New Truth?

In his book, "No God, No Science," (2013), Doctor and Professor Michael Hanby writes about the increasingly dogmatic claim that science is the sole arbitrator of truth in our culture. Today, this type of rigid, reductionist thinking is prevalent everywhere. But in the author's view, "Science without metaphysics is fiction." This is because science assumes a "there is no God" stance which renders it biased from the start. Along its way of inquiry, science continues to make "many false presuppositions about nature and God." This distorted view takes us ever closer to a mechanistic and technocratic society which pursues scientific and technological advancement above all else. In the future, these so-called scientific breakthroughs may lead to disaster if science does not stop being the de facto god of society and instead, adapts itself to the whole truth of mankind's existence. Dr. Hanby contends, "Reality is far better than all our (scientific) theories about it." Yet, he worries that as a civilization, "we are far too stupid to be this powerful." In the end, "Our hope is a God who has conquered death and the world" (quoted from Bishop Robert Barron's webinar series, "Faith and Science Summit," August 2021).

The Future of Truth

Most likely referring to our present age, Matthew 22: 24 asserts, "In fact, unless that time of calamity is shortened, not a single person will survive. But it will be shortened for the sake of God's chosen ones." Yes, we are witnessing the beginnings of a "time of calamity." It seems to be happening right before our eyes, as many people, irrespective of age, gender, religious affiliation, or geographic location, experience this "shortening" effect. In other words, our perception of time has "speeded up," and with each passing year, it seems to move ever faster (see Lesson 17, "End-Times Prophecy").

Concurrently, there will occur great evil in the world, "insomuch that, if it were possible, they shall deceive the very elect" (Matthew 24: 24). *This means that even Jesus' followers can be tricked!* Why? Because during the End-Times, deceptions and assaults on truth and justice will be so cleverly disguised, that many of "the elect" will unknowingly yield to falsehood. We actually see this happening today. The ones who remain vigilant, who steadfastly resist this invasion against truth, will have much to suffer until finally, not even they will be able to withstand the relentless onslaught. But God in His mercy will save His faithful ones, many of whom will find themselves caught in a tangled web of lies and corruption. The Lord promises to set them free and reveal His Truth to them, so they will no longer be deceived. This too, is discussed in Lesson 17, "End-Times Prophecy."

Lastly, students of these matters point to certain other biblical passages, like those found in 1 and 2 Thessalonians, which foresee a frightful conclusion to the deceitful and contentious age in which we live. These passages reiterate what has already been said: Unless our society can find a way to reject falsehood and embrace the truth, the future looks dismal indeed. 1 Thessalonians 5: 1-4, predicts disaster will come without warning: "For you yourselves are fully aware that the day of the Lord will come like a thief in the night.

Then sudden destruction will come upon them as labor pains come upon a pregnant woman, and they will not escape." There are many who believe these initial "labor pains" have already begun.

For further clarification concerning truth and the last days, I refer to the prophetic words found in Revelation 14. Verses 14 and 15 describe those "who follow the Lamb," those who are," the first fruits of God," as truth-tellers. They are lovers of His Truth, and they seek the truth above all else.

On the other hand, 2 Thessalonians 2: 10-12 warns that truth-telling will be in very short supply during the End-Times. People in general, "did not receive the love of the truth, so they might be saved. And for this reason, God will send them strong delusion, that they should believe the lie, that they all may be condemned who did not believe the truth, but had pleasure in unrighteousness." I don't know about you, but I think this prophecy is playing out now.

LESSON TEN

SEPARATION AND

REUNION

SEPARATION AND REUNION

" Those who sow in tears will reap with rejoicing.

He who goes out weeping, carrying seed to sow,

will return with songs of joy."

(Psalm 126: 5-6)

Losing Jesus

Everyone has experienced separation and loss and in their lives. Sometimes it seems to make no sense that we should lose the very thing that is most precious to us. The Gospels record that when Jesus was twelve years old, His parents realized that they had left Him behind in Jerusalem. What could be God's purpose in generating feelings of sorrow, anxiety, fear, and perhaps even guilt in those who cared about the child Jesus the most?

The scene is described in Luke 2. It shows Jesus going up to the feast with His relatives as they were accustomed to do each year. Verse 43 says that after the feast days were over, they returned, but "the boy Jesus remained in Jerusalem, and Joseph and His mother did not know it." At first, His parents thought He was with the children in their party, but after they had traveled a full day's journey, "they sought Jesus but they could not find Him" (V 44-45).

Having gone "a day's journey" before discovering Jesus was missing, is relevant to this story, as we will soon discover. Verse 45 continues, "... so they returned to Jerusalem, looking for Him." Since it took a day's journey to travel away from Jerusalem before His parents discovered Jesus was missing, it also would have taken a day's journey to return to Jerusalem. Therefore, two days had elapsed without contact with Jesus. This is also significant. Then, verse 46 reveals that, "After three days, they found Him in the Temple."

Let's look at the symbolic meaning of the narrative. First, for the Jews of that day, Jerusalem was the center of their faith, the place where God dwelt. It represents that for us too, meaning that going back to Jerusalem is symbolic of returning to God.

Secondly, as Christians, we know well the importance of three days. We recognize them as the time span between the crucifixion and death of Jesus, and His glorious Resurrection.

In Christian circles, it even has a name, "the Triduum." But do we grasp the real significance of these three days? As we know, Jesus spent two of those days in the tomb, before He resurrected on the third day. And the child Jesus was lost in Jerusalem for the same amount of time before He was reunited with His family. Could the experience of losing Jesus then, foreshadow what occurred later, during and after the crucifixion?

In comparing these two events, there are definite similarities. Each occurred in Jerusalem and during the feast of Passover. In both instances, the first two days are characterized by a period of uncertainty and confusion, while the third day provides a welcome resolution to the conflict, when Jesus is "found." In the first instance, He is discovered by His parents in the Temple on the third day. In the second instance, Jesus is "discovered" by Mary Magdalene after His glorious Resurrection.

Separation and Reunion

As I see it, Jesus' three days absence during these events establishes an essential, universal message: Separation is followed by Reunion. There is a separation, a loss, a feeling of abandonment, and at last, a joyful homecoming. Well-known Bible stories illustrate this theme. In the Old Testament, there is the legendary story of Jonah and the whale (Jonah 1-3). The New Testament includes the parables of The Lost Coin and of The Prodigal Son, recorded by Luke in Chapter 15: 8-32. Of course, the accounts of losing Jesus in the Temple and of His death and Resurrection are real events, not legends or parables, but whether symbolic stories or real life, these examples teach the same fundamental truth: Separation and loss are followed by reunion. Let's look at the symbolism of each of the three days in detail.

The First Day

The "First Day" represents an undetermined length of time. It is the time spent "in the beginning" when we take for granted many of the blessings God has given to us. Remember, in losing Jesus on the first day, none of His relatives realized He was missing. You might say they "took for granted" that He was still in their company. Indeed, no one noticed Jesus was gone until the entire day had elapsed, a time when they were moving away from Jerusalem, and away from Him. So too, most of us are not aware that we have drifted away from God. We have lost our innocence and, "We all, like sheep, have gone astray, each following his own way" (Isaiah 53:6). We do this by settling into a pattern that is comfortable and predictable, without conscious awareness that Jesus is no longer present in our lives. This is like the Jews in the gospel story; they habitually followed the same patterns of ritual and practice by making the annual pilgrimage to Jerusalem. Perhaps the trip had become so routine that they just assumed Jesus was with them, as He had always been before. Apparently preoccupied with other things, those in Jesus' traveling party failed, during the first day, to notice He was gone.

Following a prescribed set of behaviors is often dictated by the culture in which we live. It reflects our willingness to conform to the ways of the world around us. Simply observing these tendencies in ourselves can help us become more attentive to them. What lifestyle choices are we making that may hinder our spiritual growth? Are we blindly following a path that no longer serves us? Self-reflection makes us realize how much time we actually spend moving away from our spiritual goals, wasting our days on frivolous pursuits. Hence, our "First Day" is the duration of time we have spent traveling away from God. It may be shorter or longer, depending on the choices we have made as we tread our individual paths through life. Luckily for most of us, at some point along the journey, we discovered our mistake and had to admit that we were living lives devoid of meaning. In other words, we discovered that Jesus, who is the purpose and the reason for our existence, was not traveling alongside us. Only after a person is able to grasp the magnitude of this revelation, does he or she consider turning back. Interestingly, the word "repent" means "to turn around" or "to return."

The Second Day

The "Second Day" represents the start of the difficult journey back to our Heavenly Father. At this stage, we retrace our steps in order to figure out where we went wrong. Perhaps we take a personal inventory, checking to see how our time could have been better spent. This backtracking can be frustrating and discouraging because it yields no tangible results. Mary and Joseph probably experienced similar feelings as their efforts to find Jesus in their traveling party came up short. For them, the question remained: "Where is Jesus; where did He go?" For us, the "Second Day" means that we, like Mary and Joseph, have returned to the place where we started, and we too, have come up short. We find out that sincerely seeking Jesus is not the same thing as finding Him, because at this stage, He is nowhere to be found.

Returning to the Resurrection story, we see the same plot unfold. The night of Jesus's death was the start of the Sabbath which began on Good Friday at sunset. I picture the loyal band of Jesus' followers who were brave enough to witness the crucifixion, scurrying quickly home before nightfall. But what happened the day after that, on the "Second Day"? On that day they must have given full expression to their unimaginable sorrow and grief. Would they ever see Jesus again?

There is no question that our "Second Day" also feels like a time of loss and sorrow. It is a time when bewilderment and even despair can overtake us. Having come full circle, we now confront the reality that we do not feel Jesus is present in our midst. Instead, we feel alone and abandoned. It is a bit like the Gospel of Mark 4: 35-41, which tells the story of Jesus sleeping peacefully in the boat while a violent storm rages around Him and His disciples. The disciples of course, are petrified, and in a panic, they wake Jesus up. Paradoxically, it almost seems like He doesn't care; He seems undaunted by the whole thing. Similarly, Jesus may seem to be absent or "asleep" in our lives, and like the disciples in the boat, we find ourselves feeling desperate and afraid. This experience is called, "the dark night of the soul" about which St. John of the Cross wrote. It is a time when consciousness of Jesus is truly hidden from us, just as if He were asleep on the boat, or lost in the Temple, or entombed on Holy Saturday. We wonder if we will ever find Him again. Such is the anguish we feel on this day, a time of reckoning for each of us.

And as Mary Magdalene does not immediately encounter Jesus at the empty tomb, we also see that the Mother of God does not immediately find her Son during the "Second Day." In both cases, this distressing day ends in futility. It is not until the two Marys discover Jesus that the "Third Day" is set to begin.

The Third Day

This is the day the child Jesus is found in the Temple by His parents, and of course, it is the dawn of Easter Sunday, when Mary Magdalene encounters the risen Lord. Sorrow gives way to rejoicing, as Jesus reappears to those He loves.

In the case of losing Jesus in the Temple, Mary and Joseph state clearly that they do not understand why Jesus acted the way He did. By His reply, Jesus suggests that He was only seemingly lost, and He wonders why His parents anxiously sought Him (Luke 2: 49). In other words, Jesus affirms that He is "Immanuel," which means "God is with us." In some mysterious way, He has never left their side, nor ours. For us, it is only our inability to perceive Him that prevents us from experiencing His real, abiding presence in our lives.

On the "Third Day" when Jesus is found in the Temple, He comments that He must be about His Father's business. In Luke 2: 49, He expresses His intimate relationship with the Father. So, if we are to find Jesus, where must we go? We must go to "His Father's House;" this is where the Gospel of Luke tells us Jesus is. He is found, in fact, at the very center of the Temple, where the doctors and elders met to discuss the Law. Symbolically, this means we must go deep within. We do this by prayer and meditation. Not surprisingly, ancient spiritual writings have always confirmed these practices will lead us to an encounter with the Divine Presence. Even though a prayerful and contemplative lifestyle can be difficult to sustain in our frenzied world, we are urged to never stop the search or give up (2 Corinthians 4: 16). Even if we are unable to sense Jesus' presence in a tangible way, we can be sure He has never abandoned us, for He says, "I will not leave you as orphans; I will come to You" (John 14: 18). Truly, Jesus is always present at the center, the "core" of our being. Not surprisingly, the word "core" is a derivative from the Latin, "coeur," meaning heart. It is the heart which represents the "Temple" of our being where Jesus promises to meet us. This is what is meant by, "The Kingdom of God is within you" (Luke 17: 20-21). In the sixth Lesson, "Heart-Felt Prayer," I talk about how profound prayer connects us to the very Heart of God.

The words, "Losing Jesus," imply that He can be found. For He told us, "Seek and you shall find" (Matt.7: 7). Thus, the "Third Day" of our lives is experienced as a joyful reunion with Jesus! We rejoice in knowing that having faithfully sought Him, He has at last, revealed Himself to us. As we become accustomed to calling upon His Name, in both good times and bad, we find we can completely trust in His everlasting love and tender care. Thus, we come to know without any doubt that Jesus *is* present in us in a very real way. He listens to our petitions, and proof of this is - He

156

responds! We begin to see evidence of it everywhere we look. For all those who love Him, Jesus is found!

The Next Day

You might argue that our "Third Day" reunion is not really complete, since its culmination can only be fully realized in Heaven. That glorious and triumphant "Next Day" signifies the successful end of the long, arduous journey which is our lives. After our last day on earth is done, we will come face to face (1 Corinthians 13: 12). This ultimate reunion with Jesus is for all eternity! Not only that, but we will also be reunited with our loved ones who went before us, who already dwell in Heaven. The incredible promise of a jubilant Reunion is now complete!

LESSON ELEVEN

NEVER LOSE

HOPE

NEVER LOSE HOPE

" We are afflicted in every way, but not crushed;

perplexed, but not driven to despair; persecuted,

but not forsaken; struck down, but not destroyed."

(2 Corinthians 4: 8 – 9)

Fear vs. Hope

In order to understand the concept of hope, we must first look at a contrary force, that of fear. For the purposes of this discussion, fear is seen as a more obtrusive force than hope, a visceral, emotional response, one that is opposed to hope. It is an automatic, sometimes irrational, reaction to suffering, desolation, stress, and grief. If all hope is gone, nothing positive remains. Many times, the Bible speaks about fear. The word is used over 65 times in both the Old and New Testaments. So, if fear is so pervasive in the world, then we must search for its antidote. I believe hope is the only remedy; hope must take supremacy over fear. If we have genuine hope, we can say, like Jesuit author Fr. Pedro Arrupe, "I am quite happy to be called an optimist, but my optimism is not of the utopian variety. It is based on hope" ("One Jesuit's Spiritual Journey: Auto-biographical Conversations with Jean-Claude Dietsch, S.J.").

Undoubtedly, life is full of many kinds of fear; some may be imagined, while others are all too real. These fears affect all of us at some point in life, yet if we have faith, we also have hope. Psalm 34: 19 anticipates this reality with the words: "Many are the afflictions of the righteous, but the Lord delivers him out of them all." How and when He does this is not at all clear to us, so we can either accept the statement as true – in other words, have faith - or choose not to believe it.

At this juncture, I want to explore the most frequent fears we face, and what certain passages from Scripture have to say about them. I will deal with the feelings that trigger fear: persecution, anxiety, failure, rejection, distrust, food and financial insecurity, and the fear of losing control, which includes loss of health and the fear of death.

Persecution

With few exceptions, we all want to be thought well of by our fellow citizens. We want others to approve of us as human beings who have intrinsic value and self-worth, since every one of us has dignity as a person worthy of respect. Unfortunately, there are whole cultures, societies, and nations which do not hold this view; they don't even claim it as a national value. In fact, these societies repress their citizens, inflicting harm on them whenever they get out of line. Therefore, fears of political oppression, ethnic discrimination, and religious persecution are daily realities for these people. If they protest, choosing hope and the desire for freedom, they are met with violence, threatened with arrest, tortured or even killed. The righteous, all those who seek justice, peace, and goodwill, are often the ones who suffer most.

You may recall in Lesson 6, "Heart-Felt Prayer," I mention one the many famous statements Jesus made in Matthew 5, collectively known as the Beatitudes. Each of these axioms are great pearls of wisdom whereby Jesus counsels us to adopt a different, even radical, way of life, and He lists the values He wants us to live by. In the sequence, Jesus explains to us how life really is, and not how we wish it to be. Yet, He confirms the victory, for He promises we will receive a just reward for our hopeful and faith-filled efforts. One of the

Beatitudes in Matthew 5 is: "Blessed are those who are persecuted for the sake of justice, for theirs is the Kingdom of Heaven" (V 10). Psalm 34: 18 also affirms, "The Lord is close to the brokenhearted and saves those who are crushed in spirit." These verses tell us we have a God who commiserates with our suffering, but it seems the earthly struggle to overcome oppression must remain, at least for now. Indeed, this is a mystery. But a simple Google search reveals the sorry state of affairs we find ourselves in began a very long time ago. It says, "The persecution of people began in Genesis 4: 3-7 with the persecution of the righteous by the unrighteous when Cain murdered his brother Abel." So ever since that contentious beginning, those who fight for freedom and justice have been and will be assailed by fearful men. And yet people everywhere cling to hope despite the most desperate of circumstances. Jesus wants to remind all of us, "If they persecuted me, they will persecute you also" (John 15: 20).

Viktor Emil Frankl, who lived from 1905 to 1997, was a well-respected
Austrian neurologist, psychiatrist, philosopher, author, and a Holocaust survivor. His book distills what it is to find

meaning in life. In 1946 he wrote, "A Psychologist Experiences the Concentration Camp." Later the title was changed to, "Say Yes to Life in Spite of Everything," and the English translation, published in 1959, is now called, "Man's Search for Meaning." This work reveals the author's incredible resiliency in the face of the most horrific circumstances.

In another book, "They Thought for Themselves: Ten Amazing Jews" (2009), author Sid Roth dedicates a chapter to Rose Price. She lost almost all of her entire family, nearly 100 relatives, in the Nazi concentration camps. Rose was repeatedly starved, beaten, and dehumanized in every possible way. Understandably, she believed there is no God, and she especially hated Christians, equating the Germans who abused her with Christianity. But after her release from bondage and in the many years that followed, Rose came to discover the Christian God who was also a Jew. Like her, Jesus had suffered torture, but He chose to die for us all. It was a long, remarkable journey to find the Jewish Messiah from whom Rose learned forgiveness. This is what she says today: "Nobody knows the pain you have gone through, and nobody knows the pain I went through. But there is no excuse to hate. You have to forgive." If Rose can do it, maybe we can too.

Anxiety

Jesus says, "Peace I leave with you; my peace I give to you. Not as the world gives do I give it to you. Do not let your hearts be troubled or afraid" (John 14: 27). Despite Jesus' comforting words, we often experience fear as low-level anxiety and worry. Theoretically, if we were secure enough in faith, our anxieties would be manageable, but the reality is, most of us are far from that ideal. Still, Philippines 4: 6, begins with the words, "Have no anxiety at all." The entire passage is like a prayer which I like to say whenever I feel anxious or confused. And don't forget Psalm 23, which proclaims, "The Lord is my Shepherd; there is *nothing* I shall want" (V 1). These verses suggest that all of our needs are met in Christ, our Savior.

Yet even Martha, Jesus' dear friend, struggled with worry. In Luke's Gospel, Jesus addresses the matter with her because she comes to Him complaining about her sister. Martha objects to the fact that she is left to do all the household work herself, while Mary simply sits at Jesus' feet listening to His teaching. Instead of agreeing with Martha, Jesus gently rebukes her saying, "Martha, Martha, you are worried and concerned about many things; But one thing is most important, and Mary has chosen the better portion for herself, which shall not be taken away from her" (Luke 11: 41-42). In other words, you can worry and fret about things, or you can choose a higher path. You can choose to put God first, to put Him ahead of your worries, to put your trust completely in Him. I discuss the steps necessary in cultivating this attitude in Lesson 1, "The Evolution of Freewill." By trusting God with your life, no matter what difficulties arise, your inner peace and wellbeing are protected. This is Jesus' promise to those of us who get caught up in the daily stresses of life.

Jesus presents this lesson to the disciples (and us) in the parable of the Seed: He says, "The seed which is sown among the thorns refers to someone who hears the Word, but the worries of this life...choke out the Word, making it unfruitful" (Matthew 13: 22). In other words, Jesus tells His disciples that the seed of the Word of God must be planted in fertile soil and nourished if it is to grow and bear fruit. Metaphorically speaking, robust, growing seed produces a strong faith and enduring hope, both of which do not allow the cares of the world to overtake us. But if the seed is not properly sown and carefully cultivated (if it falls among thorns), it will die – and so will our faith. As our faith begins to die, so does the hope that things will work out. This is how worried, and anxiety choke out the good seed of faith. Before we know it, they creep into our consciousness, sneak into our thoughts and our hearts, and they produce fear.

The anxieties I described so far are relatively ordinary, but what if someone is suffering from a full-blown, diagnosable anxiety? In her book, "Healing through the Dark Emotions," written in 2003, Miriam Greenspan remarks, "When the ego is shattered, the heart of Love is found in this brokenness, where we least expect it." There is wisdom in this statement. It reveals the possibility that even our deepest sufferings can give way to Love (with a capital L). Here the author is talking about an ego which is not only subdued, but it has been devastated by horrific events. Whenever such a tragedy strikes - be it through illness, loss, or trauma - we can forfeit our very sense of self. Her hopeful message is that the subsequent loss of ego can be the catalyst that ignites a great spiritual awakening.

A book published in 2021 by Suleika Jaouad, called "Between Two Kingdoms," ponders this theme. The young cancer survivor writes, "And isn't that how it always goes, catastrophe forcing reinvention?" From this perspective, the brokenness a person suffers has a solution, an ultimate remedy that comes through reinventing oneself at the very core of one's being. In my opinion, if we have faith, love, and especially hope, the task will be much easier. Christians utilize these virtues to enable them to surrender their inadequacies and emotional pain to Jesus, the Loving Healer. In one of Thomas Merton's many books, "No Man Is an Island" (1955), the author writes, "Hope is always just about to turn into despair, but never does so, for at the moment of supreme crises; God's power is suddenly made perfect in our infirmity."

Failure

Failure is a painful and humiliating experience. It may be loss of a job, or failure at starting a business. It may be dropping out of college, or disappointing someone who depends on you. We fear failure because it speaks to our deepest insecurities; it exposes our inability to manage our circumstances. By using an allegory of the vine and branches,

Jesus sets the example (John 15: 2). In symbolic terms, He explains that sometimes, we need to be "pruned." This pruning can feel harsh, but just as the vine is pruned to cut away dead branches and to increase its yield, our pruning is done for our benefit. Jesus says, "This is My Father's glory, that you bear much fruit, showing yourselves to be My disciples" (John 15: 8). So, in order to bear "much fruit," we like the vine, must occasionally be pruned. Therefore, if we have failed at something, we may come to understand that the failure was a necessary "pruning." Looking ahead with hope, we pray that our failure may give rise to new and better opportunities.

By the way, it is good to remember that God's Vineyard is not only a place of pruning. It is, by necessity, a place of work and therefore, not a place of idleness. If I may extend the metaphor further, I would say there is always plenty to do tending the vines, and also getting them ready for harvest. In a real, practical sense then, every one of us is a laborer called upon to do some work in the vineyard of life. Likewise, a practical response to an apparent failure may be to look for more "fruitful" and productive work, something that gives tangible meaning and purpose to our labor.

Another thing to keep in mind about failure is this: By human standards, Jesus failed miserably in His mission. It is said, "The stone the builders rejected (Jesus) has become the cornerstone" (Psalm 118: 22). But before that marvel could happen, Jesus had to die a criminal's death, and it looked like His message died with Him. Without the Resurrection, this would have been so. Jesus describes this apparent "failure" Himself using a metaphor of a grain of wheat: "I verily say unto you, a grain of wheat remains just a grain unless it falls to the ground and dies." Only then "it produces many others and yields a rich harvest" (John 12: 24). This message is not only about the "rich harvest" produced by Jesus' death and Resurrection, but also about us too. Sometimes we have to "die" to our most cherished dreams and desires, and we are devastated; we feel as crushed as a grain of wheat. To the outer world, it looks like we have failed. Yet as I said before, such failure can bring about a whole new set of possibilities. "When they have heard the Word, they hold it fast with a good and upright heart and yield a harvest through their perseverance" (Luke 8: 15). This is the lesson Jesus teaches: we must have faith, hold on, and continue to persevere with patience until finally, it's time for the "harvest."

Rejection

Perhaps it is our family or co-workers who reject us. Their disapproval is sometimes communicated in subtle ways; other times it is quite overt. Clearly, we do not measure up to expectations, or family members fail to measure up to ours. Either way, hope of reconciliation is often lost in the milieu of hurt feelings and angry remarks. When the people we live with, or those with whom we must interact, whether at home or at work, engage in harassment and ridicule, it is easy to give up hope. We reach the point where we fear confrontation with these verbally or physically abusive people. As shown in Lesson 9, "Finding Truth," we are advised to "have nothing to do with such people" (2 Timothy 3: 5). That means we must distance ourselves from them as much as possible, and when we can't, we must try to tolerant their offensive behavior, while at the same time, we must not allow them to continue mistreating us. Easier said than done! More on this is found in the next Lesson, "Loving Relationships."

Returning to the Beatitudes, we again discover a source of consolation and reassurance. Two of the Beatitudes that apply here are, "Blessed are those who hunger and thirst for righteousness, for they shall be satisfied" (Matthew 5: 6), and "Blessed are the peacemakers, for they shall be called sons of God" (V 9). As I pondered these words, I saw how rejection is part and parcel of trying to be a more righteous person. It seems that when any of us deliberately choose the right path or head toward "the narrow gate," sooner or later an emotional reaction of rejection and desolation grips us, leaving us feeling stricken and alone. Unfortunately, rejection and all fearful conditions can render us immobile, greatly inhibiting both our material and spiritual progress. Jesus acknowledges this is a stumbling-block for many when He says, "Because narrow is the gate and difficult is the path which leads to life, there are few who find it" (Matthew 7: 13-14).

Two things are clear: One is that Jesus does not promise a resolution will occur in this life, as I explain in Lesson 2, "The Triumph of Justice." What He offers us is hope, and He asks us to cling to that hope no matter what. Secondly, Jesus Himself is our model; He suffered from ridicule, maltreatment, and rejection throughout His brief time on earth. In Luke 2: 34-35, the prophet Simeon foretells Jesus' destiny when He was born: "Then Simeon blessed them and said to Mary, His mother: 'This child is destined to cause the falling and rising of many in Israel, and to be a sign that will be spoken against. An example of the fulfillment of this prophecy is found in Matthew 13: 53 – 58: "When Jesus had finished these parables, He moved on from there. Coming to His hometown, He began teaching the people in their synagogue, and they were amazed. 'Where did this man get this wisdom and these miraculous powers?' they asked. 'Isn't this the carpenter's son? Isn't His mother's name Mary, and aren't His brothers James, Joseph, Simon and Judas? Aren't all His sisters with us? Where then did this man get all these things?' And they took offense at Him." But Jesus said to them, "'A prophet is not without honor except in his own town and in his own home.' And He did not do many miracles there." In another version of this story from Mark 6: 6, we are told that Jesus truly "marveled at their lack of faith." But besides the local rebuff He had to endure, the Pharisees and Scribes attacked Jesus constantly. He was not just unpopular, "He was a man of infirmity, despised and rejected by men. Like one from whom people hide their faces and we held Him in low esteem" (Isaiah 53).

Distrust

Sadly, many people have been mistreated in their lives, and they have developed a chronic lack of trust. Because they are emotionally vulnerable, they will not risk being taken advantage of again, and they will try to avoid any relationship that might require commitment or any kind of obligation from them. Scripture tells us we must trust God first, before we can ever hope to trust another human being. Psalm 13: 5 declares, "But I have trusted in your steadfast love; my heart shall rejoice in your salvation." When we truly trust God, we find the courage to trust our neighbor. Yes, we still risk disappointment, even betrayal; these are inescapable facts of life. But on the positive side, we learn to practice discretion, and when we have hope, we acquire resiliency. Although Jesus does not promise smooth sailing amid the storms of life, He does promise to guide our way forward if we chose to seek His help.

To sum up life's purpose, author Rick Warren says it comes down to this: "Life is a test and a trust" ("The Purpose Driven Life," the expanded edition subtitled, "What on Earth Am I Here For?" 2012). Accordingly, trust is a quality we must develop in life, but not just to trust another person; we must learn how to be trustworthy ourselves. Jesus affirms this position when He tells us to be trustworthy even in the smallest matters. For "he that is trustworthy in small matters is also trustworthy with much; and he who is untrustworthy with little, is also untrustworthy with much." Jesus continues His exposition on trust by saying, "So if you have not been trustworthy in handling worldly wealth, who will trust you with true riches? And if you have not been trustworthy with someone else's property, who will give you property of your own?" (Luke 16: 10-12). Here Jesus seems to be talking about both the bounty of earth and more significantly, of Heaven. One thing for sure, if we have been responsible, that is, if we have demonstrated our trustworthiness in earthly matters, both small and large, we are poised to inherit the vast riches of the heavenly Kingdom.

Regarding betrayal, we know that Jesus Himself experienced it. One of the twelve apostles, Judas Iscariot, refused to accept and follow Jesus' avowed mission. Nevertheless, Jesus always seemed to give him the benefit of the doubt, even to the point of allowing him to handle the apostles' communal funds. Yet Judas was unworthy of the trust placed in him, and he betrayed that trust by turning

Jesus over to His enemies for 30 silver coins. He was then arrested at Gethsemane, where Judas revealed Jesus' identity to the soldiers by giving Him a kiss (Luke 22: 1-6). I have wondered why Jesus had to be betrayed by one of His closest friends, and my conclusion is twofold: First, it was to show us that He is able to relate to and empathize with the awful pain *we* suffer from betrayal. Secondly, He permitted this cruel act because this was the only way He would perfectly fulfill the Will of the Father. To be Christ-like then, we must be willing to forgive those who betray our trust by their words or actions, even if they show no sign of remorse. This is the way *we* arrive at the gates of Heaven!

Food and Financial Insecurity

This is a global crisis which an unprecedented number of people face every day. In Lesson 3, "True Abundance," I conclude that, whatever material scarcity or lack you are experiencing, give whatever you can away. I know how naïve this sounds, but it is what Jesus requires in order to affect an increase. If you do not have any resources you can give, then give of yourself, your time and your talents. Volunteer to help those less fortunate than yourself. All the while, develop an "Attitude of Gratitude" for whatever you do have. Thank God for everything, your food, your possessions, for the very air you breathe (Ephesians 5: 20).

To illustrate the need to take initiative in this matter, I point to the parable of the Ten Talents. It offers a biblical view of how to manage our resources, be they scant or abundant (Matthew 25: 14–30). The story teaches that God rewards those who take decisive action, who use whatever they have in hand in some productive way; it doesn't matter if it is a very little or a whole lot. By this means, God alone can and will provide the increase. Remember Jesus' warning:" Whoever has will be given more, and they will have an abundance. Whoever does not have, even what they have will be taken from them" (Matthew 13: 12).

Losing Control

I remember when my mother-in-law, an independent woman named Lillian, turned eighty-five. She had acquired more than a few dents and scuff marks on her car. Sometimes, she lost her way when driving home. Finally, my husband had to make the hard decision to take away her driver's license and sell her car. To my amazement, she took it graciously, and I marveled at her willingness to let go. She remained her independent self until age ninety-two, but she never resented the restrictions that were necessarily placed upon her because of her decreasing mobility and declining health. In fact, she was always in good humor, making the best of everything life threw at her. I thought, "If only I could be that way!"

No matter what your age, loss of health can be a step toward losing control. If you have ever loved a person with advanced cancer, and watched them go through this process, you know what I mean. When it is terminal, it foretells a slow, steady decline to death. It is a journey that forces the person to let go of everything they hold dear in life. Doing it serenely seems to run in my husband's side of the family. Jim died with grace and dignity, without bitterness. In fact, he made it a point to forgive everyone who had wronged him, and to ask those he had hurt for their forgiveness. Whenever possible, he did this in person.

In Scripture we read, "He said unto Him, 'Lord, I am ready to go with you, both in prison and to death' " (Luke 22: 33). Here the apostle Peter proclaims his willingness to give up his very life for Christ. Unfortunately, he ends up denying Him three times. We too, lose our valor when confronted with fear. We are terrified by what unforeseen catastrophes might befall us. St. Paul too, was afraid and he openly voiced his fear: "My Lord," he laments, "they have killed Your prophets, and demolished Your altars; and I am left alone, and they seek my life!" (Romans 11: 3).

Death is certainly the final bastion of fear. Fearing our own mortality is of course, normal, and we can accept this reality without shame. However, it is encouraging to know that St. Paul's expression of fear quoted above, ultimately gives way to an unwavering hope, and he exclaims there is great cause for optimism. When a loved one dies, he says, "We should not grieve as others do who have no hope" (1 Thessalonians 4: 13). He does not mean we should avoid grief; St. Paul assumes we will grieve, but despite our grief, we can move forward with confidence, unlike those without hope. Not that fear is completely removed, but it is mitigated: "For God has not given us the spirit of fear; but of power and of love" (2 Timothy 1: 7). Thus, we can remain content, assured that our God is with us, faithfully watching over us as our loved one, or we ourselves, journey home. In bravely facing death, we cling to the promise of eternal life in Him (1 John 2: 25).

The Final Victory

As I have shown, there are times in our lives of utter desolation and darkness. Here again I return to Suleika Jaouad, author of "Between Two Kingdoms." She writes, "To learn to swim in the ocean of not-knowing – this is my constant work." Perhaps there comes a point for all of us when we must "learn how to swim." In Hebrews 11:1 we read, "Now faith is being sure of what we hope for and certain of what we do not see." Luckily for those who are Christian, these virtues are our "rescue buoys" that we can grab onto, and they are certainly what keep us afloat!

Indeed, as we confront the harsh realities of life, when we feel we cannot cope, it often becomes a "sink or swim" situation. This is where we who rely on Jesus, know Him as friend, companion, and guide. He beckons us, saying, "Come to Me all you who are weary and heavily burdened, and I will give you rest. Take my yoke upon you and learn from Me; for I am gentle and humble in heart, and you will find rest for your souls" (Matthew 11: 28 -29). So, in seeking a safe haven from the overwhelming demands of life, we know that, "Whoever dwells in the shelter of the Most High will rest in the shadow of the Almighty." That person will find

179

peace and safety because, "God is my refuge and my fortress; my God in whom I trust" (Psalm 91: 1-2). Having an enduring faith, St. Peter urges Jesus' followers to be ready to defend their confidence and their total commitment to overcoming fear: "Always be prepared to give an answer to everyone who asks you to give the reason for the hope that you have. But do this with gentleness and respect" (1 Peter 3: 15).

It is St. Paul who finally exclaims, "Thanks be to God! He gives us the victory through our Lord, Jesus Christ. Therefore, my dear brothers and sisters, stand firm. Let nothing disturb you. Always give yourselves fully to the work of the Lord, because you know that your labor in the Lord is not in vain" (1 Corinthians 15: 57-58).

LESSON TWELVE

LOVING

RELATIONSHIPS

LOVING

RELATIONSHIPS

" Even though my father and my mother may

abandon me, the Lord will receive me."

(Psalm 27: 10)

How Do We Love?

It is said the Gospel of John is all about love: "My children, let us not love one another in word and in tongue, but indeed and in truth" (1 John 3: 18). In modern expression, we can translate this advice as, "Actions speak louder than words!" Reading further, a passage exhorts, "Dear friends, let us continue to love one another, for love comes from God. Anyone who loves is a child of God and knows God. But anyone who does not love does not know God, for God is love" (1 John 4: 7-10). St. John continues to admonish his followers with more insightful words: "There is no fear in love; but perfect love casts out fear, because fear has anguish. He that fear is not made perfect in

182

love" (V 18).

In the previous Lesson, "Never Lose Hope," I explore how the negative, emotional impact of fear challenges and opposes our ability to hope. But here the apostle John presents fear as the most significant challenge to our ability to love. He insists that if fear occupies our minds, love cannot thrive in our hearts. Furthermore, St. John implies that if we were able to love perfectly, no fearful thought or deed could disturb our peace.

How are we "made perfect in love"? Are we to love everybody regardless of how they treat us, or how badly they behave? It seems that Scripture is asking for a total commitment to love, to love unconditionally. When Jesus proclaims the two greatest commandments, He presents "Love of God" and "Love of Neighbor" as two sides of the same coin (Matthew 22: 36-39). Verse 40 adds, "On these two commandments hang all the law and the prophets." This means that every law and rule ever written, is contingent on the command to love. A verse from 1 Thessalonians 3 encourages us to live up to the ideal Jesus taught. It says, "May the Lord make you increase and overflow with love for one another and for all persons" (V 3). That simple prayer encapsulates what our ultimate goal in life should be.

Friends

The Bible reveals God's friendship: "Greater love has no one than this: to lay down one's life for one's friends. You are my friends if you do what I command. I no longer call you servants, because a servant does not know his master's business. Instead, I have called you friends" (John 15: 13 -15). If Jesus calls us His friends, we are blessed indeed! So too, in our everyday lives, we can recognize the special blessing of having true friends. Friendship is so important that there are several scriptural passages which speak about it. From the Old Testament, Sirach 6 is an expose on the meaning of friendship. In verse 14 we read, "A true friend is a sturdy shelter; whoever finds one, finds a treasure."

There are warnings, though, not to automatically assume your friend is trustworthy. Verse 7 says, "When you gain friends, gain them through testing, and do not be quick to trust them." And in verses 10 – 12, we find this: "Others are friends, table companions, but they cannot be found in time of affliction. When things go well, they are your other self...if disaster comes upon you, they turn against you and hide themselves." My goodness, this is exactly what happened to me!

At the beginning of the COVID-19 crisis in April 2020, my husband had just passed away. We had sold the house, and I had to move 20 years of possessions out of there in a very short period of time. In the beginning, there were no family members available who could lend a hand. It felt like a tidal wave was crashing down upon me, and I admit, I was scared. Those whom I thought were our closest friends and whom I counted on for support, suddenly disappeared! And the moving company with whom I had signed a written contract, declined to honor their commitment because of the onset of the pandemic. I didn't know this until the very morning of the scheduled move when they showed up, but   then refused to load their truck. My only recourse was to cry out to God in desperation! For two days, I frantically searched for companies who would complete the move, but any who would do it were booked solid, and I was under a deadline. On the third day, the original moving company called. They said they changed their mind and would complete the move!

Not only that, but the Lord also brought new friends into my life who came to my rescue. People I barely knew and some whom I had just recently met, showed up with their pick-up trucks, food, and whatever else I needed at the moment. It was nothing short of a miracle! Here again we have the sage counsel of Sirach. Verse 16 affirms, "Faithful friends are life-saving medicine; those who fear God will find them." Verse 17 adds, "Those who fear the Lord enjoy stable friendships, for as they are, so will their neighbors be." I can certainly attest to the truth of these wise sayings. Due to my distressing moving experience, I learned the meaning and value of true friendship!

Family

One of Jesus' well-known remarks is, "For whosoever shall do the Will of my Father which is in Heaven, the same is my brother, and sister, and mother" (Matthew 12: 50). What does this statement say about our familial relationships? For as the adage goes, "Blood is thicker than water." This means, of course, that blood relationships carry more weight than all others; family must come first and be given priority over anyone else. But Jesus directs us to be more inclusive in our definition of family, as with all of our relationships. He is saying the ones who do God's Will - those people are part of our true and everlasting family.

186

For me, Jesus' mandate is clear. Since it is not my place to judge another's "worthiness," His teachings invite me to accept and welcome everyone into my family. Even if all others abandon us, Jesus assures, "I will not leave you as orphans; I will come to you" (John 14: 18). This welcoming attitude is what initially led me and my husband into foster care and adoption. Later, when our children were growing up, I recall telling them, "There is always enough love to go around." It was necessary to voice this message to them, since I could see their loyalties were divided. As adopted children, they didn't know if they could continue to love their birth parents and love us, their adoptive parents, at the same time. This problem of conflicting loyalties is at the heart of many adopted children's problems. I imagine that the same dilemma pops up in blended families as well. The solution, of course, is to be as inclusive as possible. On the other hand, I must offer a disclaimer: Sometimes there will come along a person whom you must exclude from your inner circle. Here, as always, use discernment. If there is a sense of danger or high risk involved by inviting someone into your home environment, then clearly, don't do it.

Another aspect concerning "Who is family?" comes into

the conversation here. This is the quandary presented by same sex unions. Many of these couples resort to sperm and egg donors using in vitro fertilization (IVF), or they rely on surrogate mothers to conceive a child. Consequently, a whole new family dynamic emerges. The ethical, legal, moral, and logistical problems and responsibilities associated with being the parent of one or many of these children is problematic. Indeed, the consequences of this trend may be huge, but I will not tackle them here. I will just say that at least half, and sometimes all, of the familial bonds these children normally inherit are broken. And since most of their relational ties are unknown, IVF children and those conceived from surrogate mothers may experience a vague sense of insecurity, isolation, and disconnection. How same sex parents tackle unanswerable questions such as, "Who is my 'real' grandma?" is crucial if the couple is trying to "normalize" their family life.

There is another problem created by many same sex couples. It comes with not disclosing to their IVF and surrogate children that they are not biologically related to one or both parents. If not told, these children often find out by accident or after reaching adulthood, but they do eventually find out. When they do, many of them are resentful and angry, since they feel they should have been told long before that moment arrived. By the way, this is equally true for adopted children. As a result of nondisclosure, it is likely these children, now adults, will no longer trust the one(s) who raised them. My observations are based on anecdotal information and personal as well as professional experience. Unfortunately, any long-term, lasting effects remain largely unknown and virtually unrecognized by psychology. But it is fair to say there are far-reaching implications to nondisclosure, since sooner or later, those involved will finally have to confront ambiguous and unresolved issues regarding who the 'real' relatives are. Many more questions may surface in the next generation, as a large number of IVF children reach full maturity.

When Jesus tells us to stretch our notion of family, this is what He is talking about: Include in the family circle those who are not as fortunate as we are. This means individuals who do not have family close by, or whose relatives are not emotionally supportive. Or they may have no one to visit with, or to depend upon in times of crisis. Here, Jesus' words ring true: "And the King shall answer and say unto them;

verily I say unto you, inasmuch as you have done it unto one of the least of these my brethren, you have done it unto Me" (Matthew 25: 40). We must, therefore, treat everyone we possibly can as family, just as we would treat Jesus Himself. This is why, as followers of Christ, we are called brothers and sisters. God, our Heavenly Father, wishes to unite us all in one, common inheritance as His beloved children. "And if we are children, then we are heirs: heirs of God and co-heirs with Christ - if indeed we suffer with Him, so that we may also be glorified with Him. Now if we are children, then we are heirs - heirs of God and co-heirs with Christ, if indeed we share in His sufferings in order that we may also share in His glory" (Romans 8: 17).

Enemies

"The arrogant dig pitfalls for me, contrary to your law" (Psalm 119: 85). Who are our enemies? Because I believe the devil exists as a real entity, I consider him our worst enemy. It is his influence that sabotages the efforts we make to develop loving relationships. And there are plenty of people around who are willing to play his destructive game. We know them; they are the haughty people who want to make our lives miserable. Some of them want to verbally or even physically attack us; others delight in nothing more than slandering our good name and reputation. They do this because they oppose what we stand for, so they try to bring us down. Somehow doing this makes them feel powerful. From their perspective, it strengthens their position and vindicates any wrongdoing on their part. Jesus, as always, is our guide. Suffering persecution, He endured patiently to the end. He confronted continual opposition with wisdom and serenity, except for the time He turned over the tables of the money changers in the Temple! (John 2: 15).

Ironically, the enemies whom I just described may turn out to be the very people we are called upon to love. They may be our former friends who betrayed our trust, or our estranged relatives who have mistreated us. Still, Jesus expects us to measure up to the highest degree of loving relationships. He commands us to, "Love your enemies, and do good, and lend, hoping for nothing in return; and your reward shall be great, and you shall be the children of the Highest: for He is kind unto the unthankful and to the evil" (Luke 6: 35). In Colossians 4: 6, we are instructed: "Let your conversation be always full of grace, seasoned with salt, so that you may know how to answer everyone." Going one step further, St. James has this to say, "If you show favoritism, you are committing a sin, and stand convicted before the law" (James 2: 9).

These gospel verses tell us we must not turn our backs on our enemies but try to treat them with equanimity and respect. What more are we obliged to do? Foremost, we must harbor no ill feelings against them, no matter what they are guilty of. In addition, we may wish them no harm, and we may not act out of revenge for the wickedness our enemies have inflicted. But I admit, a very attractive thought can surface in one's mind, the thought that evil should befall those who habitually cause others pain and suffering. In my normal way of thinking, I find myself entertaining the notion that, if what they did to me happened to them, it'll teach them a lesson. But you can see how short-sighted this reasoning is. That is because it never works! If irresponsible people wish to pursue a perverse and malicious agenda, the retribution they encounter is unlikely to stop them or change their way of thinking. In fact, they may suddenly turn against you with renewed vengeance. These days, it is common to see our enemies double down with their reproaches and threats whenever they encounter "push back" from us or are caught red-handed in some questionable scheme. Consequently, you may suddenly find yourself doing damage control.

Making a Difference

Recall again St. John's statement from 1 John 4: 18, "He who fears is not made perfect in love." If we agree with these words, the only option open to us is to work on overcoming our fears and perfecting our love. We read in Ephesians 4: 30-31, "Do not grieve the Holy Spirit of God, whereby you are sealed for the day of salvation. Let all bitterness and wrath and anger and clamoring and blasphemy be put away from you, together with all malice." As we struggle to do this, we eventually realize that it does make a difference on a practical level. We are less likely to get angry over trivial matters, and more likely to tolerate the foibles of friends and family. Our natural fear of reprisal or rejection may still remain, as we are not yet perfected in love. But now we don't let others' negative reactions upset us so much. Their bad behavior can no longer derail the greater quest to love.

And because we are all part of a much greater human family, we continue to seek and nurture life-giving relationships wherever we go. One way to do this is through compromise and cooperation. Another way is by just being pleasant, by bringing out the best in people with a smile, by being good-natured, kind, and patient when facing difficulty or opposition. Most often, when we can radiate a happy disposition, others follow suit, and this brings them closer to realizing that loving relationships are not only possible, but they are essential to a healthy life. St. Francis de Sales puts it this way: "We can be excused for not always being joyous, for we are not masters of joy so as to have it when we wish. But we cannot be excused for not being good, agreeable, and gracious, because this is always in the power of our will." In modern times, we have the words of Sr. Mary Rose McGeady, the current president of Covenant House, the well-known Manhattan-based home for runaway teens. Sister Mary Rose remarks, "There is no greater joy or greater reward than to make a fundamental difference in someone else's life."

He Who Has Ears

In order to make a real difference, we must be attentive to others. From Deuteronomy to Revelation, and throughout the Gospels of Matthew, Mark, and Luke, ageless biblical wisdom declares, "He who has ears, let him hear!" A Google search reports, "This is not just some generic statement for 'hey, everybody, listen up.' Rather, 'he who has ears' is every person, age, ethnicity, language, and occupation." The Google source verifies that Jesus was especially intent that people "take careful heed" to His words. Although His insistence on careful listening applies to Him, the phrase "he who has ears, let him hear" also applies to the development of all loving relationships. Put another way, if we don't pay close attention to another person's words, we may miss their meaning or worse, we may misinterpret the feelings behind them. We soon forget about being open-minded, empathetic, and inclusive, as real understanding and constructive dialogue go out the window! Although it may seem OK to respond with a shallow or half-hearted answer, what this really does is expose a lack of interest in the concerns or feelings of others.

Empathy

When Jesus commands you to *listen carefully,* He means in your everyday conversations. Besides not trying to get by with pat answers that mask your indifference, He doesn't want you to abruptly change the subject to a more socially acceptable topic just to avoid your own discomfort. When faced with another's pain, Jesus wants you to convey empathy. Listen for those times! If this is what the situation requires, then use your words. Phrases such as, "That must be so hard," or "I can't imagine how you are feeling right now," or, "What can I do to help?" go a long way to ease a distressed person's anxiety level. At other times, the right thing to do is patiently listen, and that alone can make a huge difference. One thing for sure, if you decide to enter into the conversation in the first place, you must be fully invested in it. Ironically, a different problem occurs if you are too invested in the conversation. That's when your own self-interests dominate; you are constantly interrupting and talking too much, not giving anyone else the chance to speak. Or perhaps you are prone to engage in gossip. Obviously, these approaches prevent the careful listening Jesus requires. In the above scenarios, it is evident that failure to *really pay attention and appropriately respond* is the real culprit.

A final aspect of this discussion is the ability (or inability) to apologize when confronted with a situation where something went wrong. The simple, humble gesture of saying, "I'm sorry," or "Oh no, I didn't realize..." or some similar phrase is facing extinction in today's culture! Yet, statements like these can so easily mitigate a problem. What most people don't recognize is that an apology is the most direct route to rectifying a conflict when somebody's feelings have been hurt (although it was surely not intentional). An apology is always a *humble* response; a prideful person would never respond this way. In the final analysis, we must put good, effective communication tools into our toolbox and use them. Doing so will help make all our personal interactions more productive and pleasant. This in turn, will foster the creation of loving and meaningful relationships in our lives.

Do What You Say

When it comes to giving in the material sense, we are invited to do so generously, for "each one must give as he has decided in his heart, not reluctantly or under compulsion, for God loves a cheerful giver" (2 Corinthians 9: 7). But if you choose to give, never do it grudgingly. Instead, as in all loving relationships, "Let your yea be yea; and your nay, nay; lest you fall into condemnation" (James 5: 12). In other words, when you say "yes" to do something, mean "yes;" and when you say "no," mean "no." Always make your intentions clear from the onset, one way or the other, so as to avoid misunderstanding or argument. And if your answer is "yes," then you must follow through wholeheartedly with what you have committed to do.

Jesus tells a parable about two sons to illustrate the importance of honoring your commitments. In the story, one son tells his father he will not do the work his father asks of him, but later he changes his mind and does it. The other son promises to do the work, but in the end, he does not do it (Matthew 21: 28-31). Jesus asks the crowd, "Which of these two did the will of his father?" When they reply, "The first one," Jesus remarks, "Truly I say to you that even the tax collectors and harlots will precede you into the Kingdom of God!" By this stern rebuke, Jesus was accusing them of insincerity. What His parable conveyed to the crowd is this: Do not make loud professions of faith for the sake of expediency, so your words are praised and admired, but when put to the test, you renounce that very faith. And equally important, do not make solemn oaths and false pronouncements before others, when you have no intention of following through on your commitments (V 32). To use a contemporary phrase, Jesus tells the people of His time (and us) to "Walk the Talk!"

Alone and Together

There seems to be a delicate balance between our need for people and our desire to be alone. If we are with others all the time or rely on them too heavily, we can become co-dependent, overwhelmed, or scattered. If we are alone too much, we may feel lonely, depressed, or become insular, that is, closed off from anything outside our narrow scope of activity. To strike a healthy balance can be difficult at times. We know the early disciples of Jesus lived in small communities along with others who were His followers. They shared what they had, possessing everything in common, and they especially ministered to the poorest among them (Acts 2: 42-45). Today, churches everywhere follow this pattern. They launch programs for the homeless, provide soup kitchens, operate schools, hospitals, and nursing homes, run prison programs, and participate in many other forms of service and charitable work.

So although we no longer live in "a" community of believers, we still live "in" community with others. This model affords a practical way of life; it balances our need for alone time with an active life, participating in meaningful work as our livelihood, or attending to the needs of family, friends, and others. Both inward and outward expressions are essential if we are to foster loving relationships; the first mode of expression is done passively, while the second one is done actively. Time spent in solitude allows us to develop a keener sense of who we are and what we have, as well as what others lack. This is how we acquire a commitment to be of service. It is then we decide to go out into the community, investing our "time, talents, and treasure" in worth-while projects and causes. Doing this not only helps others, but it reinforces our need for fellowship, giving us an opportunity to "move outside ourselves," to stay connected by actively participating "in" community. At the same time, this very participation can drain us. Whenever that happens, we must withdraw periodically in order to revitalize and renew our enthusiasm and commitment. Most often, this special time is spent alone on family vacation, or on retreat with others. Any time experienced apart from the normal routine is always time well spent. The interlude gives rise to a fresh outlook, providing unexpected insights leading to new, creative ideas that facilitate problem-solving.

It's About Love

In the end, it is all about love. Of course, there are people we encounter "out there" who seem unlovable. Yes, they can be irritable, rude, or ultrasensitive; being around them is like walking on eggshells. No matter what we say or do, they harbor negative feelings, are likely to hold a grudge, and they don't seem to want loving relationships in their lives. I gave one such example in Lesson 3, "True Abundance." But despite the barriers people like this put up, it behooves us to be as patient, gentle, and as kind-hearted as we can be. We must always try to give of ourselves as much as possible, without the intrusion of anger, resentment, or selfishness, so that the goodness and love of God may manifest in the world. Romans 13: 8, says it this way, "Owe no one anything expect to love one another." For in the end, our existence is all about love. Everything else will ultimately pass away; only love will remain. Expressing that love in the world is what we are, what we are made for, what loving relationships are all about.

LESSON THIRTEEN

GAINING

WISDOM

GAINING WISDOM

" If any of you lacks Wisdom, he is to ask God, who

gives to everyone generously and without

rebuke or blame, and it will be given to him."

(James 1: 5)

The Wisdom of Solomon

What is wisdom? When we look to the Bible for answers, it defines wisdom in different ways depending on what verses you may be reading. But attaining wisdom is really about the quest for meaning and purpose, for beauty and truth. From a biblical standpoint, we gain wisdom as we come to realize the countless gifts of creation as God-given, and that things put on earth are here to provide for our sustenance, to comfort and assist us in times of need. From this point of view, gaining wisdom means gaining spiritual insight into the infinite value and significance of each human person in the eyes of God. In the Book of Sirach, Chapter 17: 5, the prophet says, "He (God) created of him a helpmate like to himself: He gave him a mind to counsel, and a tongue, and eyes, and ears, and a heart to devise: and He filled him with *the knowledge of understanding."*

So, from the very beginning, the acquisition of knowledge was an integral part of God's plan for humanity. Wisdom was so revered in ancient times; this prized possession came to occupy its own special place in religious literature. According to Wikipedia, there are seven Sapiential or Wisdom Books of the Septuagint, or the Greek Old Testament. For the purpose of this discussion, I chose three of these books to review; collectively they are known to us as, "The Wisdom of Solomon." The first book is called, "Proverbs," the second is, "Ecclesiastes," and the last book is called, "Song of Songs." Their author is purported to be King Solomon himself, and in his day, he was considered the wisest of men.

You will find all three books in the present-day Bible. My Catholic edition contains an additional book called simply "Wisdom," also ascribed to Solomon, and "Song of Songs" is called, "Canticle of Canticles." As a primary reference, I am using the work of Henry M. Morris, "The Remarkable Wisdom of Solomon" (2004). Following the author's lead, I will give a brief summary of the three books in the order they appear in the Bible. And I will look at what relevance the axioms contained in Proverbs and Ecclesiastes, and the allegory, Song of Songs, may have for us today.

Proverbs

In the book of Proverbs, there is an impressive list of universal sayings. Scholars believe King Solomon wrote and collected them over his entire lifetime. The first nine proverbs are thought to be wise admonitions which Solomon wished to impart to his son, Rehoboam. In the next group, from Proverbs 10 to 22, there are 375 individual sayings, composed as stand-alone words of wisdom. According to my reference source, the last section of Proverbs, Chapters 23 through 31, contain various pronouncements addressed to different people and written at different times. I will share a small sample from each group, but before I begin, it is important to note that the sayings found here may appear trite or "old school" to the modern reader. Nevertheless, they still ring true today, and you will see why they retain their significance.

From the first group, I picked Proverbs 1: 7: "The fear of

the Lord is the beginning of knowledge; but fools despise wisdom and instruction." Today it can be argued that the ignorance of those who do not "fear of the Lord" is evident everywhere. This verse contends it is foolishness to try to possess true wisdom and knowledge without first respecting God. Verses 8-14 continue with advice to Solomon's son and to all young people in general. They speak of the importance of heeding the standards and instructions of parents, with the assurance that doing so will lead to a full and productive life. Solomon's wise counsel instructs young people to perceive the snares that are set for them, before they get caught in them. Verses 20 through 33 are one long complaint, lamenting that many refuse to listen to the wisdom Solomon has presented to them. Finally, verses 30-33 predict their demise: "They would none of my counsel; they despise all my reproof. Therefore, shall they eat of the fruit of their own way, and be filled with their own devices. For the turning away of the simple shall destroy them, and the prosperity of fools shall slay them. But whoso harkens unto me shall dwell in safety and shall be quiet from fear of evil." Thus, Solomon admonishes the youth of his day to attend to his words, words that are good counsel for all youth, both then and now. These timeless proverbs insist that young people everywhere must strive to live in accordance with righteousness; Solomon declares that the safety of divine Providence is granted to those who adhere to his sage instruction. Advice such as this is a reoccurring biblical theme, as shown in Lesson 5, "Choose Life."

As we read on, the sayings in Proverbs continue to extoll the immeasurable value of wisdom, the true Wisdom which ultimately comes from God. King Solomon himself had asked God for this gift at the beginning of his reign, and it had granted him (1 Kings 3: 13). The remaining proverbs contained in the first group are about classic moral values. "My son, despise not the chastening of the Lord; neither be weary of His correction: for whom the Lord loves He corrects; even as a father the son in whom he delights" (Proverbs 3: 11-12). "Envy not the oppressor, and choose none of his ways," for "the curse of the Lord is in the house of the wicked; but He blesses the habitation of the just" (V 31-33). Chapter 6, verses 16-19 assert, "These six things does the Lord hate; yea, seven are an abomination unto Him: a proud look, a lying tongue, and hands that shed innocent blood, a heart that devises wicked imaginings, feet that be swift in running to mischief, a false witness that speaks lies, and he that sows discord among brethren." For more on this topic, see Lesson 9, "Finding Truth."

When we get to Chapter 8 in Proverbs, verse 10 again advises, "Receive my instruction in preference to silver, and knowledge rather than choice gold." More sage guidance follows, and by the time we arrive at Chapter 15, the remaining verses refer to a variety of unrelated topics and situations. In this chapter, the first line reads, "A soft answer turns away wrath; but grievous words stir up anger." Verse 33 comments, "The fear of the Lord is the instruction of wisdom, and before honor is humility." Chapter 16: 16 declares, "How much better is it to get wisdom than gold! and understanding rather to be chosen than silver." As is often the case, Solomon uses the symbolism of silver and gold to extoll the brilliance of the supreme knowledge he has attained, for he considers it more valuable than the most precious of metals.

The following verses are general admonitions. In Proverbs 16: 32-33 is the axiom, "He that is slow to anger is better than the mighty; and he that rules his spirit (is better) than he that takes a city." The first line of Chapter 19 instructs, "Better is the poor that walks in integrity, than he that is perverse in his lips and is a fool." In Chapter 20: 4, we read, "The sluggard will not plow by reason of the cold, therefore shall he beg at harvest, and have nothing." Chapter 21: 1 presents a poetic rendition of Solomon loyalty to the Lord. He proclaims: "Likes streams of water, so is the King's heart in the Hand of the Lord; He turns it wherever He will." This beautiful passage shows Solomon's heart and mind, that is his will, is aligned with God. He further counsels, "Every way of a man is right in his own eyes; but the Lord ponders the hearts" (V 2). The special role of the heart is explained in Lesson 6, "Heart-Felt Prayer."

As we continue in Proverbs, Solomon teaches, "He who follows after righteousness and kindness finds life, prosperity, and honor" (Chapter 21: 21). As an adjunct to this advice, he counsels forgiveness: "Say not, I will do so to him as he has done to me; I will render to the man according to his work" (Chapter 24: 29). Adding to these remarks, Chapter 25: 21-22 gives more direction: "If your enemy be hungry, give him bread to eat; and if he be thirsty, give him water to drink. For you shall heap coals of fire upon his head, and the Lord shall reward you." This particular sentiment made its way into New Testament writings where it appears in Romans 12.

Lastly, I will highlight Proverbs 28: 1, which affirms, "The wicked flee when no man pursues them, but the righteous are confident as a lion." By these words Solomon reminds us that if we maintain integrity and remain just, we can stand firm; we can be steadfast, bold, and courageous, as "confident as a lion." Although these sayings may strike you as quaint, they represent ideals which we still aspire to today. This is the reason they continue to appear in modern editions of the Bible. The wisdom they offer is meant to empower us, and just as in ancient times, these words ask us to reflect upon our understanding of how and why mankind must act, so that in the end, our conduct will be "counted as righteousness" (James 2: 23).

Ecclesiastes

According to biblical scholars, the book known as Ecclesiastes is considered Solomon's "swan song," that is, a final work he composed in the latter part of his life, like a last will and testament. In these verses, Solomon speaks a lot about vanity and the futility of all human wisdom. But before we get there, you may recognize from Ecclesiastes 1: 9, a well-known axiom: "That which has been is that which will be, and that which has been done is that which will be done. For there is nothing new under the sun." In the next few lines, Solomon elaborates on this theme, but he takes note that for those who are unwise, "There is no remembrance of former things" (V 11). Another, more famous passage in Solomon's writing forms the basis of the popular song, "Turn, Turn, Turn." The verses are found in Chapter 3: 1-8, which begins, "To everything there is a season, and a time for every purpose under Heaven."

Regarding vanity, Solomon remarks, "I have seen all the works done under the sun, and behold, all is vanity and vexation of spirit" (Ecclesiastes 1: 14). Reflecting on this, Solomon is not content. He says, "And I gave my heart to know wisdom, and to know madness and folly: I perceive that this also is vexation of spirit. For in much wisdom is much grief; and he that increases knowledge increases sorrow" (V 17-18). An interpretation of this decline into melancholy comes from author Henry M. Morris, whose book I referenced earlier. The author believes that when King Solomon wrote Proverbs, he was speaking confidently about attaining wisdom, which he saw as synonymous with the fear of God. But when Solomon wrote Ecclesiastes, he was an old man who was dismayed by the "pseudo-wisdom and secularized knowledge" he witnessed around him. Furthermore, in Ecclesiastes, Chapter 2, Solomon goes on to decry the fact that he did all he could to satisfy every earthly desire he had, and yet, "There was no profit under the sun" (V 11). Here he concludes that his vast wealth and earthly possessions could never generate happiness. Lastly, Solomon comments that upon his death, when his riches go to another, "Who knows whether he be a wise man or a fool? Yet shall he have rule over all my labor wherein I have labored, and wherein I have showed myself wise under the sun. This is also vanity" (V 19).

The last chapters of Ecclesiastes are said to be the greatest. This is because they are an exhortation regarding the vanities of youth, and the inevitability of old age and death. In Chapter 11: 9, Solomon tells the young men of his day that after all the things they will do in life, always remember, "God will bring thee to judgement." He continues in Chapter 12, "Then shall the dust return to the earth as it was; and the spirit shall return to God who gave it. Vanity of vanities says the preacher; all is vanity" (V 7-8). In verses 9-14, Solomon acknowledges the merits of his contribution to wisdom, but although he saw it was good, he laments, "Much study is a weariness of the flesh" (V 12). Finally, Solomon declares, "Let us hear a conclusion to the whole matter. Fear God and keep His commandments; for this is the whole duty of man" (V 13). Verse 14 ends with, "For God shall bring every work into judgement, with every secret thing, whether it be good or whether it be evil." This statement ultimately reduces the value of everything worldly to nothing, with the stipulation that only goodness and wickedness will remain to be judged. In summation, Solomon admits to the inscrutable actions of God, declaring that they will always be a mystery. Chapter 8: 17 exclaims, "Then I beheld all the work of God. Though the wise man thinks to know it, yet shall he not be able to find it out."

Song of Songs

The third book I present in this collection is Song of Songs. It is about Solomon's love for his wife, Naamah, who became the mother of their son, Rehoboam. On the surface, this is an idealized tale of their romance; it is a charming and beautiful love poem. But most biblical scholars concur that the verses are to be read and interpreted on an allegorical level, which carries as much meaning, or more meaning, than the literal text. That is to say, Song of Songs should not be read simply as depicting Solomon and Naamah's passionate love for one another. Instead, as allegory, the story is understood as the perennial search for God. More on this later.

Throughout this book, Naamah's incredible beauty and virtues are praised; she is hailed as "the fairest among women." In most of the verses, Solomon makes use of similes to describe Naamah's loveliness. We see her compared to fine horses; her cheeks and neck are as rows of jewels and golden chains (Chapter 1: 9-10). Verse 15 continues, "Thou art fair, my love; behold thou art fair, thou hast doves' eyes."

In Chapter 2, it is Naamah herself who speaks. She also uses similes to describe herself: "I am the rose of Sharon and the lily of the valleys" (Song of Songs 2: 1). She continues, this time expressing her ardent love, "As the apple tree among the trees of the wood, so is my beloved among the sons. I sat down under his shadow with great delight, and his fruit was sweet to my taste" (Chapter 2: 3). Here, she waits for her lover to arrive, and upon hearing his voice, she responds immediately (V 8). He says to her, "Rise up, my love, my fair

214

one, and come away. For lo, the winter is past, the rain is over and gone" (V 10-11). Much sensory imagery follows, the turtledoves are singing, and the lovely scent of flowers fills the air (V 12-14).

In Song of Songs 3: 1-5, we witness the bride-to-be undertaking a desperate search throughout the city where, she laments, her lover has gone. After some time, Naamah finds him, and when she does, "she would not let him go" (V 4). Following this joyful reunion, the preamble to their marriage begins with elaborate preparations. It is certainly an extravagant affair, and no expense is spared: "King Solomon made himself a chariot of the wood of Lebanon. He made the pillars thereof of silver, the bottom thereof of gold" (V 9-10). The next chapters speak of Solomon's immense devotion to Naamah, and of his profound desire for her to be his bride. His words are lavish and gushing with feeling. He begins, "Thou hast ravished my heart" (Chapter 4: 9). He extolls her purity, referring to her as "a garden enclosed, a fountain sealed." But soon she will become "a well of living water," once she has become his bride (Chapter 4: 12).

In the next chapters, Naamah shares with "the daughters of Jerusalem" her undying love for her bridegroom (V 8). She talks in similes, "His hands are as gold rings set with beryl, his belly is a bright ivory overlaid with sapphires" (Chapter 5: 14). In Chapter 6, Naamah again addresses her bridegroom's departure, but now she realizes, "her beloved one has not really forsaken her, nor is he lost somewhere. It is just that he is temporarily away on other important duties." (Quoted from "The Remarkable Wisdom of Solomon," by Henry M. Morris, 2004).

In Chapter 7 of Song of Songs, Naamah performs a wedding dance before Solomon. He is captivated by her beauty, and again uses similes to express his awe of the rapturous elegance of his bride. The story progresses and their marriage is consummated. In Chapter 8, we find Naamah has persuaded her husband to go back home to visit her family. But the couple is not well received. Finally, the reproaches have been worked out, and the bride's family accepts the business arrangements that were made for caretaking the vineyards. In the concluding verse of Chapter 8, the bride is calling her beloved to come to her once more, now that her personal obligations have been settled. Naamah joyfully exclaims that she is completely free to be with him now. In verse 8, she asks Solomon to, "set me as seal upon your heart, as a seal upon your arm; for love is stronger than death." Naamah beckons him to affirm their bond forever.

An Allegory

The story of "Song of Songs" presents Naamah as the Bride-to-be. From the perspective of allegory, she represents all true seekers of the Lord, recognized today as the universal Church. She goes out actively searching for her Bridegroom, but she does not initially find Him. The Bridegroom, of course, is Jesus Himself. Naturally, while her Beloved is away, the Bride is heart-broken and she pines for His return. Like Naamah, the Church has also experienced barren episodes in her history when God seems absent from her midst. But despite these periodic setbacks, she, like Naamah, has persevered. Here we can see how the Bride's intense longing for the return of her Beloved portrays the Church's unquenchable desire for her Spouse, Jesus Christ. The story ends happily; it is an expression of the archetypal theme I describe in Lesson 10, "Separation and Reunion." In the final chapter of the narrative, the newly married pair goes out to ensure the vineyards are properly cared for. We may note that at first, they are not well received by the caretakers. We can compare this to Jesus and the Church "going out together" to attend to the needs of those who would reside under their care and protection. But like the young couple in the story, they (Jesus and His Church) often meet with fierce opposition despite benevolent intentions. Nonetheless, as the narrative suggests, all is well in the end.

In studying the allegory, we recognize that throughout the centuries, the Bride of Christ, the Church, bears the awesome responsibility to answer the perennial call of her Beloved. As she strives to do this, the story reminds us that we, as lovers of God, will ultimately find Him whom we seek, and we will attain everlasting happiness with Him. This viewpoint is put forth and explored in a remarkable book called, "Song of Songs: The Soul and The Divine Beloved," by John Davidson (2004). The truth of this study shows the allegory has significance for us; it portrays God's faithful and unending love for His Church, whom He will rescue, redeem, protect, and finally make His own at the end of time.

In order to understand this sublime love, imagine for a moment the most idealized form of love you can fathom. Now realize that this love is just a shadow of Jesus' love for His Church. This love is all-consuming, and it is purer and sweeter than any human love, beyond anything we can

218

grasp! The Song of Songs narrative expresses this unquenchable love in poetic imagery, and by doing so, it foretells what we will experience in Heaven! There, we will be immersed in the divine marriage which is union with Christ, and we will partake of the royal banquet (Isaiah 25: 6). When we experience Jesus' love in Heaven, it will be so overwhelmingly beautiful and intimate that we will be totally captivated by it. This is why we are not given in marriage in Heaven (Matthew 22: 30). Jesus is our one, true, loyal, and everlasting Spouse. Abiding forever in Him, we are satiated with love to the extent that no other needs are possible. Thus, Song of Songs inspires us; it allows us to catch a glimpse of the transcendent relationship we will have with God once we are fully united with Him. In the meanwhile, during our time left on earth, we continue to search for and return to Him, for He is the glorious Source of eternal joy - Jesus, our Divine Spouse.

Lessons for Today

In summary, the first two books from "The Wisdom of Solomon" provide timeless sayings offering wise counsel, while the third book is an allegorical story of passionate love. Together, the collection reveals a wisdom which is not new, for "There is nothing new under the sun" (Ecclesiastes 1: 9). Rather, "The Wisdom of Solomon" imparts, like all great literature, an ageless quality to recall and ponder, a standard of conduct to measure up to. Here we recognize the universality of human experience, for we are given a truth that is equally applicable to all ages and times. Here too, we identify the same axioms civilizations and all great religions of the world share, value, and profess to uphold. These truths, recorded by King Solomon so long ago, can still provide a road map for us today.

LESSON FOURTEEN

COME

HOLY SPIRIT

COME HOLY SPIRIT

" You will be given power when the Holy Spirit

comes upon you; then you will be my witnesses... to

the very ends of the earth."

(Acts 1: 8)

Who is He?

For me, the concept of the Holy Spirit has always been elusive. In Christian parlance, He is also known as the "Holy Ghost," but in recent times, the words "Holy Spirit" are used more frequently to describe Him. We can understand from Scripture that this Spirit is intricately connected to the Father and the Son; each are separate Persons, yet one God. But who is He exactly and what role does He play? Because of the limitations of language, using the pronoun "He" to describe the Spirit (which has no gender) is both awkward and arbitrary. Truly, it is hard to picture the Holy Spirit as an individual at all; does He have feelings and a personality? As strange as it seems, this mystery cannot simply be dismissed or explained away. The

Holy Spirit is real, but He can only be apprehended by those who have personally experienced Him actively working in their lives.

St. Catherine of Siena once said, "The Father is your Table, the Son is your Food, and the Holy Spirit waits on you and then makes His dwelling in you." This imagery is helpful if we are to understand the dynamic interactions of the triune God, or Holy Trinity. St Catherine's description implies that the Spirit acts like a liaison; this is so we may receive the divine sustenance prepared by the initiative of the Father and the Son. St. Paulinus instructs us, "God produces His love in His people through the Holy Spirit whom He pours out upon all flesh." This means the Holy Spirit is the essence of love, and *no one* is excluded from receiving this gift! St. Bernard of Clairvaux makes a point of stating that God cannot be known only "through books and lectures," but through intimate experience, "the way one friend knows another." He adds, "That knowledge is what the Holy Spirit facilitates" (quote taken from Bishop Robert Barron's "The Word on Fire" Bible, 2020).

A Definition

Let's look for a further explanation of who the Holy Spirit is for the Christian church. The Catholic Catechism gives a concise answer as recorded below. It must be noted however, that there are numerous variations of this basic understanding which flourish side by side within Christianity. As Scripture may be interpreted in different ways, so too, the Holy Spirit may be felt and experienced differently, depending upon cultural norms and a plethora of global religious attitudes and beliefs.

According to the standard Catechism:

> To believe in the Holy Spirit is to profess faith in the Third Person of the Most Holy Trinity who proceeds from the Father and the Son and is worshipped and glorified with the Father and the Son. The Spirit is "sent into our hearts" (Galatians 4: 6) so that we might receive new life as sons (and daughters) of God (reference numbers 683-686).
>
> In the indivisible Trinity, the Son and the Spirit are distinct but inseparable. From the very beginning until the end of time, when the Father sends His Son

He also sends His Spirit who unites us to Christ in faith so that as adopted sons (and daughters), we can call God "Father" (Romans 8: 15). The Spirit is invisible, but we know Him through His actions, when He reveals the Word to us and when He acts in the Church" (reference numbers 687-690 and 742-743).

From this vantage point, we recognize that the Holy Spirit works like a mighty wind: Most often He can be felt, but not seen. When we witness evidence of His action, it is similar to how we observe the wind blowing through the trees, watching as it rustles through the leaves. In addition, the above source confirms the Holy Spirit's personhood. As a Person, He can be known and worshipped as God. Lastly, we recall that Jesus was conceived without a human father through the power of the Spirit. Therefore, the Virgin Mary is said to be the Spouse of the Holy Spirit since His action in her predicated the Divine conception. These elements provide a solid foundation, so we may proceed with clarity.

As the Catechism states and Scripture verifies, Jesus is God in equal measure with the Father and the Spirit. First, we can say while on earth, Jesus possessed the Father, for He announced, "I and the Father are one" (John 10: 30; also John

14: 10-11). Secondly, Jesus possessed the Spirit, as revealed in this passage: "Jesus being full of the Holy Ghost returned from Jordan and was led by the Spirit into the wilderness" (Luke 4: 1). Moreover, we read in Matthew 3: 11 that John the Baptist gave witness to the Spirit residing in Jesus when he said to the crowd, "I indeed baptize you with water unto repentance, but He that comes after me is mightier than I, whose shoes I am not worthy to bear. He shall baptize you with the Holy Ghost, and with fire." And after John baptized Jesus, "Suddenly the Heavens were opened, and he saw the Spirit of God descending like a dove and resting on Him." Then the voice of the Father spoke as thunder from Heaven saying, "This is My beloved Son, in whom I am well pleased. Listen to Him" (Matthew 3: 16- 17).

Outward manifestations of the Spirit can be felt just a dramatically today. Those who encounter Him may be found at healing prayer meetings, worship services, and Pentecostal revivals. Catholics experience the movement of the Spirit when partaking of the sacraments, especially the Holy Eucharist. Sometimes we sense the Spirit's presence as we immerse ourselves in deep prayer. When we are in a prayerful and meditative state, He may reveal Himself as a

226

still, small voice, such as Elijah experienced (1 Kings 19: 11-12). In all cases, the immensity of the Spirit's action is felt in a visceral way, and it cannot be ignored or denied by the person experiencing it.

The Comforter

Jesus explains, "Nevertheless I tell you the truth; it is expedient for you that I go away: for if I go not away, the Comforter will not come unto you; but if I depart, I will send Him unto you" (John 16: 7). Jesus's departure at His Ascension into Heaven was apparently vital to release the power of the Holy Spirit into the very heart of the early Christian community. I have often wondered why this was so. I wanted Jesus to remain on earth forever! Somehow though, it was right and proper, indeed essential, that forty days after the Resurrection, Jesus ascended and took His place at the right hand of the Father (Luke 22: 69).

Continuing with the Gospel of John, in Chapter 16, verses 12-14, Jesus gives the disciples further counsel about the Holy Spirit: "I have much more to say to you, more than you can now bear. But when He, the Spirit of Truth, comes, He will guide you into all the truth. He will not speak on His own; He will speak only what He hears, and He will tell you what is yet to come. He will glorify Me because it is from Me that He will receive what He will make known to you."

Undoubtedly, Jesus' final departure left a huge void in the lives of those who followed and loved Him during His time on earth. Therefore, it was a great consolation to them that Jesus foretold He would send the Comforter, the Holy Spirit, whom He also identified as the Spirit of Truth. After His Ascension, Jesus kept the promise He made to His followers. In preparation for this momentous event, He had given them specific instructions on what to do, basically telling them to gather together, to pray, and to wait. The Book of Acts, Chapter 2, describes what happened on the day of Pentecost. It was then the Holy Spirit revealed Himself as tongues of fire which fell upon each person present. "And they began to speak in various languages according to whatever the Spirit gave them to speak" (Acts 2: 4). The important thing to remember here is that the disciples had prepared well for this moment; their hearts and minds were of one accord. Thus, they were fully equipped to receive God's gift of the outpouring of the Holy Spirit.

For us today, it is the same. We must prepare ourselves

spiritually so that we are ready to receive the amazing gifts that the Holy Spirit wishes to impart. Jesus tells us how to access the Spirit; He says we must ask: "If you then, being evil, know how to give good gifts unto your children: how much more shall your Heavenly Father give the Holy Spirit to them that ask him?" (Luke 11: 13).

1 Corinthians 12: 3 tells us, "No one can say Jesus is Lord, except by the Holy Spirit." Nevertheless, while all Christians believe that the Spirit comes to dwell in them at baptism, many lose awareness of Him altogether later in life. So when asking God to impart the Spirit's gifts to us, we must not be presumptuous. 1 Corinthians 7: 19 warns, "Or do you not know that your body is the temple of the Holy Spirit that dwells within you, which you have of God, and you are not your own?" Since many are ignorant of this, they may ask for the extraordinary gifts of the Spirit and not receive them. The biblical injunction not to defile the body must be observed first, since it is a necessary prerequisite for the Holy Spirit to manifest. Truly, when it comes to the exceptional gifts the Spirit imparts, we observe they are given to a select few, only to "whosoever keeps His (Jesus') commandments." These special individuals "will be guarded by Him, and He will

dwell in them. And by this we know that He abides in us, by the Spirit which He has given to us" (1 John 3: 24).

According to Revelation 3: 21-22, Jesus speaks to His followers: "To the one who overcomes, I will give the right to sit with Me on My Throne, just as I overcame and sat down with My Father on His Throne. He who has an ear, let him hear what the Spirit says to the churches." In this passage, Jesus invites those who have overcome sin to sit with Him. What a magnificent invitation; Jesus places His friends right alongside Him in Heaven! Then He says that the revelations He gives are communicated through the Holy Spirit, and it is our duty to stay informed about what the Spirit is saying. This is because these revelations are given to the "churches" and the churches, of course, are us!

Gifts of the Spirit

There is much talk among Christians today about the necessity of receiving the gifts of the Holy Spirit. What are these gifts? "The fruit of the Spirit is love, joy, peace, patience, kindness, goodness, fidelity, gentleness, and self-control" (Galatians 5: 22). But among the Protestant denominations, there seems to be a preference for a particular gift of the

Spirit, that of speaking in tongues. This is the phenomena of speaking in foreign or strange languages, just as happened on Pentecost. Today, many feel this gift is the most important one to receive, and there are several gospel verses ascribed to St. Paul which support this notion. 1 Corinthians 14: 2 says, "Through the Spirit he speaks mysteries," thus confirming that praying in tongues allows access to a profound depth of spiritual knowledge which cannot be accessed otherwise. For the one who receives this gift, it may mean he or she acquires the ability of precognition or prophecy and is given power over certain situations and conditions. This gift has a name; the recipient has received, "A Word of Knowledge."

Despite the emphasis on this particular form of witnessing, the Gospels tell us that, just as the Spirit comes in many forms, He also brings many different gifts, implying that all of them are equal in value in the eyes of God: "But the manifestation of the Spirit is given to everyone as a help to him. For to one there is given through the Spirit the message of wisdom, to another the message of knowledge by the same Spirit, to another faith by the same Spirit, to another gifts of healing by that one Spirit, another the working of miracles, to another prophecy, to another distinguishing between spirits, to another speaking in various tongues, and to still another the interpretation of tongues. But all of these gifts are wrought by that one and the same Spirit, dividing to every one as He will. For as the body is one and has many members, and all the members of the body, even though many, are one body, so also is Christ" (1 Corinthians 12: 7-12). As I see it, our job is to step aside and allow the Holy Spirit free reign to work in us, doing so in whatever manner the Lord sees fit. Thus, we will receive the particular gifts He wishes to grant us.

Anointing

Baptism in the Holy Spirit is sometimes referred to as an "anointing." We read in 1 Corinthians 1: 21-22, "Now it is God who has confirmed us with you in Christ, and *who has anointed us*, and who has sealed us, and pledged His Spirit in our hearts." To understand what "anointing" all is about, I turned to the website, "What Christians Want to Know:"

> The apostle John said that Christians, "have an anointing from the Holy One, and all of you know the truth" (1 John 2: 20). Who is this Holy One? 1 John 2: 27 gives us more on this anointing, "But the anointing

that you received from Him abides in you, and you have no need that anyone should teach you. But as His anointing teaches you about everything and is true, and is no lie—just as it has taught you, abide in Him. "Who is the bringer of the knowledge of God? This "anointing" teaches us about "everything" and it abides in us. So, it appears that the Holy Spirit is this anointing, and if a person is a believer in Christ, they have this anointing with the presence of the Holy Spirit who abides in them. Therefore, all believers are anointed by the indwelling of the Holy Spirit. Some can walk more closely in the Spirit, but there is not a believer that does not have the Holy Spirit, for if you don't have the Holy Spirit, you are none of Christ's (Romans 8: 8-11).

As stated above, all Christians believe that at their baptism, they received the Holy Spirit. Perhaps by virtue of this baptism alone, we qualify to receive more powerful "anointings" later on, once our faith has matured. Indeed, there is evidence in the Bible that the Holy Spirit manifests His presence in a mighty way at various times in the course of a person's spiritual development. This fact accounts for the powerful testimonies given by faith healers, Christian ministers, and by the thousands of people whose lives they have touched. Today, Evangelical and Pentecostal leaders loudly proclaim that they have been anointed by the Holy Spirit in new and profound ways, as by fire, in order to fulfill a particular divine mission. It certainly may be true that some of the popular, media-driven Evangelicals are nothing but frauds, and their only mission is to lead others astray and to line their pockets with donations. Nevertheless, not all of them can be dismissed as charlatans. As I said before, once you see and feel the palpable movement of the Holy Spirit, it is hard to deny; His powerful presence becomes irrefutable evidence that God is active in our lives today.

Faith and Spirit

Ephesians 1: 14 says, "When you believed, you were marked in Him with a seal, the promised Holy Spirit who is the first installment of our inheritance until the redemption of those who are God's possession." Wonderful! In faith, this seal was given to us as a "first installment," guaranteeing our place in the Kingdom of God. Although this is true for every baptized person, a saint from the third century, Cyril of Jerusalem, explains that the greater our faith is, the greater the presence of the Spirit within us: "Though the remission of sins is given equally to all, the communion of the Holy Spirit is given in proportion to each man's faith." This may explain why those most devoted to Jesus often have a special affinity for perceiving the Spirit's action in their lives. Such sensitivity allows them to recognize His divine revelations, and these individuals are always deeply moved when they experience this mighty but sometimes subtle, force. Over the centuries, the power of the Holy Spirit is responsible for the many well-documented physical and spiritual healings we know about today.

Remarkably and paradoxically, those who remain skeptics may, under certain conditions, spontaneously experience the Holy Spirit. When these exceptions occur, they are often marked by incredible, awe-inspiring events whereby the dynamism of the Holy Spirit is on full display. I think experiencing this power depends entirely upon the receptivity of each individual person at the time of their exposure to it. Jesus reminds us to *always* remain open and receptive to the call of His Spirit, especially since that call sometimes comes in the least likely place, to the most unlikely person, at the most inconvenient time. That is why we are asked to become like little children. Only little children are humble enough to accept what comes their way without censor or bias. Therefore, as adults, Jesus tells us we must be willing to put aside our fascination with intellectual pursuits, our stubborn attitudes and opinions, and our inflexible lifestyles in order to glimpse, with child-like awe, a new reality, to perceive with a different kind of seeing. Jesus comments, "Therefore, whoever takes the lowly position of this child is the greatest in the Kingdom of Heaven. So anyone who becomes as humble as this little child is the greatest in the Kingdom of Heaven." (Matthew 18: 4). It is therefore true that any humble, sincere person who can look with the eyes of a simple child, may experience the workings of the Holy Spirit. And anyone who can attune their ears to hear that "still, small voice" within, will hear it speaking to them today. The question is, are we listening?

236

LESSON FIFTEEN

AUTHENTIC

MIRACLES

AUTHENTIC MIRACLES

" This beginning of Miracles did Jesus in Cana of Galilee and manifested forth His glory; and His disciples believed on Him."

(John 2: 11)

Miracles

Miracles can be loosely defined as events or occurrences that have no logical explanation. In our scientific age, miracles have been soundly debunked, since many insist there is a natural explanation for all things mysterious; and in the cases where there is uncertainty, we just haven't found the right scientific answers yet. Ironically, St. Augustine saw it the other way around; he said not reason first, but faith: "Therefore seek not to understand that you may believe – but believe that you may understand."

Because it can be argued that some "miracles" are merely the result of natural phenomena, this notion is often used by skeptics as "an easy out." That is to say, if they can come up

238

with a plausible explanation that may account for a miraculous event, then it is no longer deemed miraculous. Such a proposition is put forth to explain the parting of the Red Sea, which allowed Moses and the Israelites to escape Pharaoh's armies during their Exodus from Egypt (Exodus 14). The reasoning is that the Red Sea parted naturally as a result of the underwater shelf that still exists there; this is the spot where the Jews supposedly crossed. At that particular time, the sea receded naturally to expose the sandbar underneath, making it possible for the Israelites to flee to safety on the other side. The theory further explains that the sea naturally closed off this escape route during high tide, right in time for all of Pharaoh's charioteers to drown while in hot pursuit. It sounds like a flimsy argument to me, but many logical minds will go to great lengths to discredit the belief that miracles existed then, and that they continue to exist today.

To circumvent this issue, I chose to review four special miracles which scientifically speaking, are deemed irrefutable. This is because over many years, they have undergone intensive, rigorous scrutiny. First, I will highlight the Shroud of Turin, secondly, the Tilma of Our Lady of

Guadalupe, next, two Eucharistic Miracles, and lastly, the question of Incorruptibility.

The Shroud of Turin

This is perhaps the most studied artifact of all time. Christians believe it is the burial cloth of Jesus, and on it appears the full body image of a crucified man. The Shroud is 14 feet 3 inches long, and 3 feet 7 inches wide, since it covered the back of the body as well as the front. Over the years, there have been claims of forgery. One such finding purported to show that the cloth itself was medieval in origin. This fact alone would discount it as a fraud. Later though, further investigation revealed that the piece of cloth taken for the sample happened to be from a section where repairs were made by nuns in 1532, after the Shroud was rescued from a fire. In 2000, researchers Marino and Benford presented a paper called, "Evidence of the Skewing of the C-14 Dating of the Shroud of Turin Due to Repairs." This paper presented the actual facts of the case, and with it came renewed interest and more precise research, which has been underway ever since. Modern textile studies now date the cloth at 33 BC, give or take 250 years in either direction. It is further understood that if an ordinary man had been interned in the Shroud, his decomposing body would have emitted fluids which would have decayed and utterly destroyed the fabric centuries ago. Such is not the case. These facts make it more convincing than ever that the cloth is what it is purported to be: the authentic burial cloth of Jesus Christ.

Everything about the Shroud has been scrutinized: the pollen on the cloth and the 3:1 herring style of linen, what appears to be a crown or cap of thorns, the scourge marks on the back of the body, and the placement of the nails on the wrists just below the palms. Then there are the Roman coins, known as Pontius Pilate Leptons, which were placed in the eye sockets. But most notable of all, are the unique qualities of the image itself, which is likened to a photographic negative. Indeed, the image was not discovered until photography was invented and with it, the use of negative plates. As a negative image, its existence would not have been discovered at all without the advent of photography.

Today, scientists speculate that the image on the Shroud could only have been caused by something like "a short-term radiation burst." According to researcher Marino, who has investigated the Shroud for over forty years, such an image cannot be duplicated using current laser technology. There is also undeniable evidence that the image is not painted or dyed, since the image is not "in" the cloth as would be if this were the case. Conversely, the radiation that caused the image is on the very surface of the cloth, on the inside of it which is the part that would have made direct contact with the body. In 2010, Italian scientists attempted to replicate this radiation induced image by employing an excimer laser. They were unable to do it. Likewise, to date, no credible evidence has surfaced which would expose the Shroud as a fake. The consensus among researchers is, indeed, this is the burial cloth of the historical Jesus. Yet podcasters are quick to say that the Shroud, although miraculously conceived, does not "prove" the Resurrection of Jesus. How so? If He did indeed rise from the dead, isn't the Shroud exactly what you would expect to find? For more on this subject read, "Wrapped Up in the Shroud," by Joseph G. Marino (2020).

The Tilma

In 1531, Juan Diego was a poor indigenous peasant living in an area close to what is now Mexico City. He was a humble man of the Chichimeca people. As a convert to Christianity, he would rise early in the morning to attend church some distance away. On one such trip, he met a beautiful lady, who told him to tell the bishop to build a church on the spot where she indicated. Although Juan tried to convince church authorities of his heavenly vision, he was not believed. Finally after several attempts, the bishop asked Juan to give him a supernatural sign as proof. What the Lady did next was truly miraculous. She told Juan to go pick roses on a hillside in a place she showed him, even though it was the beginning of winter and he knew no flowers grew there. Juan obeyed anyway and went to gather the roses. Then, another greater miracle occurred after Juan returned to the bishop, carrying the roses in his tilma or cloak. As he opened his garment, with the roses cascading to the floor, the people in the room were aghast. Most spectacularly and to everyone's sheer astonishment, the Lady's image was miraculously imprinted inside Juan's cloak!

This image, now known as Our Lady of Guadalupe, still exists today. It is displayed and venerated at the Basilica of Santa Maria de Guadalupe in Mexico City, where countless pilgrims from all over the world come to view it each year. On May 6, 1990, Juan Diego was canonized a saint by Pope John Paul II.

One of the things considered miraculous about Juan's

tilma is the condition of the fabric, which has remained intact throughout the centuries. Unfortunately, in more recent times, the invention of electric lights and the cumulative effect of smoke from centuries of candle burning and incense have taken their toll on the tilma's condition. Nevertheless, scientific research proves no paints or dyes were ever used in the creation of the image found there. Modern investigations reveal that the mantle Our Lady is wearing reflects the position of the stars in the sky at the time the apparitions took place. And with the aid of the latest technologies, it can be shown that the eyes of Our Lady of Guadalupe emanate a reflection as would occur naturally. These eyes actually reflect the people who were in the room at the very moment when the tilma was opened! A written document from that day records the event and verifies the identities of those who were present. Yes, these same people can be seen in the reflection of Our Lady's eyes as the actual personages there! This suggests that at that instant, the Virgin Mary herself was present in the room through her miraculous image. By 1541, just ten years after Our Lady's appearance to Juan Diego, a historian of the period records that nine million indigenous people in Mexico had converted to Catholicism! Thus, the people of an entire country abandon their pagan gods and found truth by way of this spectacular event.

Eucharistic Miracles

The Eucharist is what Christians call "Holy Communion." Standing on a firmly established theology, Catholics believe that the bread and wine we receive as Communion is not a symbol of Christ's body and blood. Instead, through a divine intervention known as "Transubstantiation," the priest consecrates the gifts of bread and wine, transforming them at that moment into the *actual* body and blood of Christ. This is what or rather who, we receive in Communion, for we believe Jesus is truly present in the "species" of the consecrated bread and wine.

Hebrews 9: 11-14 explains how the ancient Jewish ritual of animal blood sacrifice was replaced and supplanted by Jesus' offering of Himself. The fiat of the sacrifice of the "Unblemished Lamb" meant that He conquered physical death once and for all, thereby giving eternal life, redeeming everyone who will accept the truth of His Passion, death, and Resurrection. To understand the concept of Transubstantiation then, is to understand the enormity of what Jesus did. To put it in laymen's terms, you might say that because Jesus willingly offered Himself as the Supreme Sacrifice and was victorious over sin and death, He now has unlimited authority and power. This means He can transform Himself into whatever appearance He wishes. So for our sake, in giving Himself to us in Holy Communion, Jesus takes on a simple form, disguising Himself as it were, in the appearances of bread, which is given as a round "host," and wine. If you have any doubt about this, just look at His own words, because Jesus told His followers He would do just that:

The event is recorded in John's Gospel. At the time, we observe an unruly crowd which is repulsed and outraged by Jesus's statements. He tells them bluntly, "I am the bread of life" (John 6: 48). What could He possibly mean by this? The crowd is further scandalized when Jesus answers them, "If any man eats this bread, he shall live forever; and the bread which I will give is my body, which I am giving for the sake of the life of the world" (V 51). And Jesus does not stop there. He goes on to declare, "Unless you eat the body of the Son of man and drink His blood, you have no life within you…He who eats my body and drinks my blood has eternal life, and

I will raise him up on the last day. *For my body is real food, and my blood is real drink"* (V 53-55). Here Jesus confirms that He Himself is truly present in the bread and wine which is consecrated or set apart for the sacred purpose of our receiving Him in Holy Communion. But at the time Jesus made this outrageous declaration, it was altogether too much for the crowd to bear. Many went away disgusted by His words. When Jesus saw this, He asked His disciples, "Do you also want to leave Me?" From then on, even some of His most loyal followers distanced themselves from Him (V 64).

Later at the Last Supper, the twelve apostles witness the actualization of Jesus' radical statement. Here's what happened: Jesus first tells them He is about to sacrifice His life for the remission of sin. Afterwards, when they had finished the meal, "and when He had given thanks, He broke the bread, and said, 'Take, eat *this is My body*, which is broken for you: do this in remembrance of Me. After the same manner also He took the cup, when He had supped, saying, *this cup is the New Testament in My blood*: do this, as often as you drink it, in remembrance of Me' (1 Corinthians 11: 17-34). Throughout the centuries until today, we not only recall the events of the Last Supper at every Catholic Mass, but we also receive the consecrated body and blood of Jesus in the very same manner in which Jesus' apostles did. If believers fully appreciated the significance of partaking in this sacrament, exclaimed former Pope and saint, John XXIII, "How copious would be the fruits of harmony, peace, and spiritual decorum that would flow therefrom for the Church and the whole world!" As you will see in the last part of this essay, Pope St. John XXIII is one of two saints whom I feature in the discussion on Incorruptibility. The Council of Trent made the doctrine of Transubstantiation an official dogma of the Catholic Church in 1551.

After the Reformation brought about by Martin Luther in 1517, the ensuing Protestant split from Catholicism created a controversy concerning belief in the phenomenon of Transubstantiation. Martin Luther held that "It is not the doctrine of Transubstantiation, which is to be believed, but simply that Christ really is present at the Eucharist." As a result of this ambiguous statement, what today's Protestant denominations believe about Holy Communion varies. Generally speaking, Lutherans do not believe in the real presence of Jesus in the sacrament, while Methodists and Episcopalians do. But Catholic theology concerning this matter has always remained firm. St. Thomas Aquinas tells us that God's glory and goodness emanate from the Eucharist. "Hence, those who approach the Divine sacrament obtain God's glory much more than those who abstain from receiving it." This declaration must be true because the fact of the Transubstantiation is proven through accounts of Eucharistic Miracles, documented throughout the history of the Catholic Church.

From the earliest report recorded in Lanciano, Italy during the eighth century, to the most recent Eucharistic Miracle in Poland in 2013, these miraculous events are verifiable realities. What happens during these episodes? It is nothing less than the consecrated Eucharistic bread (in the form of a round host) and the wine actually change form. The Eucharist visibly changes into human tissue, into recognizable heart muscle, and the wine into human blood. A book by Joan Carroll Cruz, called, "Eucharistic Miracles," chronicles many of these amazing, inexplicable events. In the eighth century account, the miracle occurred when a priest-monk was celebrating Mass. The priest had secretly entertained doubts about the real presence of Jesus in the sacrament. At the moment of consecration, "The host was suddenly changed into a circle of flesh, and the wine was transformed into visible blood. History records that after the miracle was certified, a document telling the details of the miracle was written on parchment in both Greek and Latin and was safeguarded by the monks." Today, an ivory reliquary holds the relics which remain preserved at the monastery.

In 1970, the latest of numerous authentications took place, "in a most scientifically complete manner," according to Ms. Cruz. She reports that, "The flesh was identified as striated muscle tissue of the myocardium, having no trace whatsoever of any materials or agents used for the preservation of the flesh." She goes on to report, "Both the flesh and the sample of blood were found to be of human origin, emphatically excluding the possibility that it was from an animal species." The specimens were not hermetically sealed, but "they were not damaged; although they had been exposed to the influences of physical, atmospheric, and biological agents." In other words, as time passes, relics such as these stay remarkably fresh; they do not decay or decompose in any way.

As stated, there are more recently documented cases

which have been meticulously examined, reexamined, and finally authenticated by independent scientists. For those which occurred after Ms. Cruz wrote her book in 1987, the most advanced technologies were employed to ascertain the exact composition of the substances involved. I will share the results of one such analysis done for the 2013 event. This is the Eucharistic Miracle which occurred during the celebration of Christmas Mass **at** St. Hyacinth's Shrine in Legnica, Poland. As the faithful were partaking of communion, a consecrated host accidently fell to the floor. Following the Church's protocol to respect the sacred species, the priest placed the host in a container of holy water and kept it in the tabernacle (this is the place on the altar where the hosts are kept). Two weeks later, the priest discovered that the host had turned red. He reported this to the bishop and a commission was established to observe the phenomenon. At the end of the inquiry, the bishop released a statement regarding the official Forensic Medicine Department's analysis. The findings conclude, "In the histopathological image, fragments of tissue were found, which contained fragmented particles of striated muscle tissue. The whole image... is very similar to that of a cardiac muscle...that shows changes typical of an agony. DNA shows that the tissue is of human origin." The significance of this is huge! "The agony" described in the report means that the tissue sample is from that of a *living* person who has been tortured but is not yet dead. In other words, the heart tissue under investigation has been subjected to extreme stress, a degree of stress that is indicative of the final phase preceding death. Experts agree that an event of this type is impossible to manufacture. Likewise, the Eucharistic Miracles which have been subject to the most rigorous types of scientific inquiry, all exhibit the same astounding characteristics. The only conclusion possible is that Jesus is truly present in the Eucharist, continuously offering us the sacrifice of His very life!

Incorruptibility

When a person has been dead for some time, their body may be exhumed because of a request made for reburial. But also, it may be done as part of a formal investigative process which is required by Christian tradition to move a holy person closer to being officially declared a saint. Under normal conditions, an ordinary body naturally decomposes. However, there is a phenomenon called, "Incorruptibility" which evidences the fact that in hundreds of well documented cases, the exhumed bodies of deceased, soon-to-be recognized saints, have been miraculously preserved from normal decay after death. In these cases, mummification and all other forms of artificial preservation have been considered, investigated, and ruled out. Joan Carroll Cruz, the same author of "Eucharistic Miracles," also wrote a book in 1977 about this strange anomaly which she titled, "The Incorruptibles." Here she relates the stories of 102 saints whose remains are recognized by the Catholic Church to be incorrupt. First, I will highlight one well-known example from Ms. Cruz's book, St. Bernadette. The other, which is too recent to be found in the book, is the case of Pope St. John XXIII. The quotations I cite in the first case are taken from the book.

At Lourdes, France, there is a world famous, sacred shrine where the Blessed Virgin Mary appeared to a very poor peasant girl named Bernadette in 1858. She was not only poor, but she also suffered from asthma, and failed at her studies. As a young girl, Bernadette was entrusted to the care of the Sisters at Nevers, and at age 22, she entered their religious order. Although always sickly, Bernadette worked periodically as a sacristan and at the infirmary. Her illness was aggravated by tuberculosis of the bone with many complications, until her death at age 35 at the convent. Bernadette's body was exhumed thirty years later. When the tomb was opened, two doctors and the sisters of the community were present. No odor came from the remains of the saint, and according to a report written at the time of the event, the body was found to be "completely victorious over the laws of nature." It had retained its natural skin tone and texture, and "her perfect hands held a rosary which had become rusty." In 1919, a second exhumation took place. This time, because the well-intentioned nuns had washed the body during the first exhumation ten years prior, the face had become slightly discolored. Everything else was as before. Today the incorrupt body of the Saint of Lourdes can be viewed at the Chapel of St. Bernadette, located at the motherhouse in Nevers, France.

The second case, that of the late Pope St. John XXIII, is described in an excerpt from an article written in April, 2003 by Renzo Allegri. It describes the celebratory events marking an anniversary commemorating the Pope's death. This was a special occasion however, since the next Pope, John Paul II, decided to move the incorrupt body of his predecessor from its original resting place below the church of St. Peter's, to a place of prominence and honor in the central part of the Basilica which is located at the Vatican in Rome:

An emotional crowd paid homage to Pope John XXIII whose remains were displayed in St. Peter's Basilica on June 3rd, the thirty-eighth anniversary of his death. It seemed as though time had stood still. People flowed emotionally past his body, just as in 1963, during the three days prior to his funeral. Then, Pope Angelo Roncalli (the birth name of John XXIII) had just died. Now, thirty-eight years have passed since his death, but his face is just the same: serene, almost smiling, and perfectly preserved. The fact that his body had remained incorrupt for 38 years after his death made headlines all over the world when it was discovered on January 16th of this year. Pope John was beatified on September 3rd of last year (this is a formal step toward sainthood). He was born in Sotto il Monte in the province of Bergamo, Italy and enjoyed great popularity during his lifetime.

255

He continues to be well loved even after his death. His tomb, which used to be in the crypt of St. Peter's, has always been the site of pilgrimage for the devout, who have increased in number after his beatification. For this reason, Pope John Paul II decided that the remains of his illustrious predecessor be placed in a tomb in St. Peter's Basilica, so people could find it with greater ease.

Today, anyone can visit the Basilica and view the incorrupt body of the saint, Pope John XXIII.

An Eternal Incorruptibility

In summary, miracles remind us to hope in something far greater than the capacity of human understanding. The miracles presented in this short essay attest to the fact that something supernatural is clearly going on. Furthermore, anyone can capture a glimpse of it if they are willing to take a serious look. Imagine, if people would open their minds and hearts to the possibility of miracles, how much better the world would be! All miracles point to the same truth; that there is a loving God, and those who faithfully follow Him see miracles happen in their lives.

In a vision of heavenly glory, the apostle Paul catches sight of the ultimate victory: He says, "In a flash, in the twinkling of an eye, at the last trumpet; for the trumpet will sound, the dead will be raised imperishable, and we will be changed. For the perishable must clothe itself with the imperishable, and the mortal with immortality. When the perishable has been clothed with the imperishable, and the mortal with immortality, then the saying that is written will come true: "Death has been swallowed up in victory. Where, O death, is your victory? Where, O death, is your sting?" (1 Corinthians 15: 52 – 55). This is certainly a promise worth striving for!

LESSON SIXTEEN

HEAVENLY

SIGNS

HEAVENLY SIGNS

" And God said, 'Let there be lights in the expanse
of the heavens to separate the day from the night.
And let them be for Signs and for seasons, and for
days and years."

(Genesis 1: 14)

Signs

What do I mean when I talk about signs? Well, when you see a sign in everyday life, it literally points you in the right direction. A supernatural sign does the same thing. We see these signs as moments of clarity, synchronicity, and revelation that may surprise or even astound the person experiencing them. This is because they often come out-of-the-blue, at unexpected times and in unexpected ways, spontaneously without any pre-thought. Yet just as often, a person may hold a deep yearning to receive a specific sign which he or she is then predisposed to receive. Make no mistake, these signs are from God, and because they are, they provide consolation and hope. When they are received, they always empower the receiver, allowing the person to move forward with courage during what may be a very trying time in life. The experience can be likened to driving down a dark, winding road at night. It is only when you turn your high beams on, that the road ahead emerges with clarity. Another analogy is trudging through a dense forest. At first, there seems to be no trail in sight, no way out. Then all of a sudden, a clear path appears ahead. This is what signs are like!

There is no doubt that some things happen purely by chance. That is to say, they are not signs of anything. But although coincidences do occur, so do signs. In other words, some things are coincidences, but some things are not. So how do we distinguish between a true sign and something that is merely coincidence? First of all, whether it occurs spontaneously or as a result of a heart-felt plea, a true sign is difficult to ignore. Once you have attuned yourself to the possibility, a sign moves you to the core. Nonetheless, I realize that in our skeptical world, the tendency is to write off such moments; we just dismiss them because we are too busy to actually reflect on what they could mean. However, if we decide to stop and remain receptive for a moment, we will recognize the transcendent nature of signs, and by doing so, we can allow their gift to penetrate our consciousness.

The second thing we need to pay attention to is their frequency. A sign may come as a singular event, or it may be repeated over and again "until we get the message." If the thing in question appears to be nothing other than an ordinary, common place occurrence, then perhaps it is just that, and it reveals nothing at all. However, if the event is rare, or occurs repeatedly despite the odds, and especially if it is the specific sign that was asked for, then there is probably something to it. Lastly, we can experience signs as dreams. For one famous saint, John Bosco, heavenly signs always came in the form of dreams. These dreams helped him navigate the difficult path of educating poor and neglected street children, both in corporal and spiritual matters. For him, dreams were literally signposts along the way, since they gave him specific information and warnings concerning what lay ahead. Frequently, they indicated the perilous state that the souls of some of the boys in his care were in. Once informed, St. John Bosco would always take immediate action to rectify the matter in whatever way he could. This information is from, "Forty Dreams of St. John Bosco," compiled by Fr. J. Bacchiarello, S.D.B. (1969).

In all cases, that is, in all the different ways signs can appear, it is important to pay close attention to them. For the thousands upon thousands of people who do, signs are life-giving; their gift is that they offer a path to resolution, inner peace, consolation, and hope. The ethereal effect of a sign is like a heavenly balm of grace, especially in the face of trials, hardship, or grief. Generally, signs can be divided into three categories: There are signs that Guide our path, those that are Warnings or Premonitions, and those that act as positive Reinforcement or Confirmation, offering a resolution to a vexing problem, question, or decision. A single, poignant sign may serve one, or a combination of these purposes. For instance, the sign may be understood as guidance, but also as a warning. If ignored, it could become a premonition of some unforeseen danger ahead. This is why it is important to take the signs that come to us seriously. In the next segment, I will show how signs operated and were recorded during biblical times. Then, I will identify some contemporary signs of our times, and finally, I will review some of the personal signs I have received. For easy identification and to highlight the word, I have capitalized the "S" in the word "sign" when discussing the significance of these events.

Biblical Signs Concerning Jesus

In the Old Testament of the Bible, there are many instances where miraculous Signs appeared to herald what was to come. They range from mystical dreams to concrete physical Signs. Here I wish to concentrate on a few heavenly Signs which foretold the coming of Christ. One such Sign is found in Micah 5: 2. It points to the place where the Messiah, the much-anticipated King of the Jews, would be born: "But you, Bethlehem Ephrathah, though you are small among the clans of Judah, out of you will come for me One who will be ruler over Israel, whose origins are from of old, from ancient times." This passage admonishes the Israelites to anticipate the appearance of Jesus, the long-awaited Messiah, from the likes of Bethlehem, a relatively obscure and unsavory place. The circumstances surrounding the birth in Bethlehem were in themselves additional Signs, affirming the fact that the heavenly infant had been born there.

The prophet Isaiah offers his testimony when he reveals, "Therefore the Lord Himself will give you a Sign: Behold, the virgin will be with child and give birth to a Son and will call

Him Immanuel" (Isaiah 7: 14). Later in Chapter 11: 1-2, the prophet foretells, "There shall come forth a shoot from the stump of Jesse, and a branch from his roots shall bear fruit. And the Spirit of the Lord shall rest upon Him, the Spirit of wisdom and understanding, the Spirit of counsel and might, the Spirit of knowledge and the fear of the Lord." These passages act as testimonies or Signs predicting the virgin birth and the child's royal ancestry. Joseph, who was the earthly father of Jesus, was indeed a direct descendant from the noble lineage of the House of David. The Messiah's royal bloodline was also confirmed by the prophet Hosea (Hosea 3: 4-5).

"When the designated time had come, God sent forth His Son born of a woman" (Galatians 4: 4). At this moment, a spectacular Sign is seen in the sky. Three Kings from the Orient, the Magi, were expert astrologers. When they observe the brilliant star, unlike any they had seen before, they are compelled to follow it. This Sign, which must have been an incredible sight, leads the Magi to where the holy infant lay. But before they get there, they inquire of Herod, the reigning Jewish King, what he knew about this heavenly Sign. Herod consults his own "wise men" and determines that the future

King of the Jews, the Messiah, would indeed, be born in Bethlehem (Matthew 2: 3-8). So Herod commands them, "When you find Him, tell me so that I, too, may go and worship Him." Herod's actual motive was to apprehend the child and kill Him since this new King posed a real threat to his rule. But the Magi receive a second Sign; they are "told in a dream not to return to Herod, so they depart to their own country by another way" (Matthew 2: 12).

At the same time, another Sign heralding the Jesus' birth is given to simple shepherds who were watching over their flocks on that glorious night. From Luke's Gospel, Chapter 2, verses 12-16, we read that an angel appears to announce the news, proclaiming: 'And this shall be a Sign unto you; you shall find the babe wrapped in swaddling clothes, lying in a manger.' And suddenly there was with the angel a multitude of the heavenly host praising God, and saying, 'Glory to God in the highest, and on earth peace, good will toward men!'

I have noted only a few of the Bible's recorded Signs signifying Jesus' arrival into the world. Sid Roth, the author and founder of the "It's Supernatural!" website, asserts that the Hebrew prophets had received hundreds of Signs pointing to the coming of the Messiah. Unfortunately, the people of the day did not recognize the time of their visitation and they refused to accept the truth of what was foretold. As it turned out, there were consequences for ignoring these Signs. In Luke 19: 44, Jesus predicts the total destruction of Jerusalem which would occur in 70 AD: "They will dash you to the ground, you and the children within your walls. They will not leave one stone on another, because *you did not recognize the time of God's coming to you.*" In other words, the people repeatedly rejected the many Signs they had been given and they failed to recognize Jesus when He came (John 1: 10).

After the Magi depart, Joseph, the humble spouse of Mary, has a dream. As we've seen, dreams are often the vehicles by which important messages are conveyed. In the dream, an angel instructs Joseph: "Get up, take the child and His mother, and flee to Egypt, and remain there until I tell you; for Herod is about to search for the child and destroy Him" (Matthew 2: 13). The Holy Family leaves immediately. They escape by night, just as Herod orders the murder of all baby boys born in and near Bethlehem during the past two years.

Missed Signs

Despite the Signs the Jews had received, and the many miracles Jesus performed, they steadfastly refuse to believe in Him (with the exception of a small band of followers who became the first Christians). Ironically, the people of Jesus' time are still seeking after Signs that they think will somehow convince them if He is really their anticipated Messiah. Jesus, however, would have none of it: "A wicked and adulterous generation seeks after a Sign, and there shall be no Sign given to it, but the Sign of the prophet Jonah" (Matthew 16: 4). Jesus goes on to explain, "For just as Jonah was three days and three nights in the belly of the great fish, so will the Son of Man be three days and three nights in the heart of the earth" (Matthew 12: 40). Here we see a parallel between the story of Jonah who was consumed by a whale, and the three days Jesus spent enclosed in a tomb before rising from the dead. Put another way, Jonah's experience had been a Sign which foreshadowed Jesus' death and Resurrection, a Sign which was utterly rejected by the Jews of the time. To paraphrase, Jesus is saying, "If you have not understood the Sign of Jonah and the many other Signs you were given by the prophets, you are unlikely to believe Me now either." For more about Jonah, see Lesson 7, "Practice Vigilance."

Jesus makes His argument crystal clear with a parable about a poor leper and an unrepentant rich man, both of whom die. At the end of the story, the rich man wants to go back to earth to warn his brothers about his horrible fate after death. In other words, he wants to rise from the dead in order to alert them. However, he is told, "If they do not listen to Moses and the Prophets, they will not be convinced even if someone were to rise from the dead" (Luke 16: 31). That's a pretty harsh statement, isn't it? Jesus uses this story to bring home the point; He Himself will rise from the dead, yet as He predicts, the people still will not believe. Why? Because they were not going to believe no matter what! That is the startling lesson of this parable spoken by Jesus to the incredulous and defiant crowd.

Truly, Jesus is outraged by the unbelief of the people. He expresses His frustration in John 5: 45-47 where He exclaims, "What! Do you think that I will accuse you before the Father; there is one who will accuse you, even Moses in whom you trust. For if you had believed in Moses, you would also have believed in me; for Moses wrote concerning Me. If you do not believe his writings, how then can you believe My Words?"

Signs for Our Times

Jesus exhorts His listeners to be vigilant and ready. In Matthew 24, for example, He gives both warnings and predictions about the future. However, some prophetic verses are veiled in mystery, as is the Book of Revelation, the last book of the Bible. Suffice it to say that Jesus warns His followers to watch closely for the Signs of the times: "From the fig tree, learn a parable. As soon as its branches become tender and bring forth leaves, you know the summer is coming. So even you, when you see all these things, know that it has arrived at the door" (V 32-33).

What are some specific Signs of the times we can investigate today? Among scholars who study these things, quite a few maintain there are seven Signs which predict the arrival of the End-Times and the second coming of Christ. A website called, "End-Times Bible Prophecy" details these seven events, and I will list them below. When all of them have occurred, it will signal we have entered an era unparalleled in human history. I will not include many details here, since you can refer to this and other websites for details. It must be noted though, circulating around the internet are many diverse views about the sequence and types of events which will take place. Therefore, please consider the list below as just one opinion from one website. Another source is the book, "Seven Signs of the End-Times," by Britt Gillette. The author presents a slightly different take on the seven events, but they point to the same end result. For the purpose of researching contemporary Signs as prophecy, I definitely consider the Seven Signs worthy of further study:

The Holocaust and the Re-Emergence of Israel

One of the preeminent signs of the end times is the Jewish survival of the Holocaust and the re-emergence of the nation of Israel as a Jewish state. In Ezekiel 37: 11-13 we read, "Then he said to me, 'Son of man, these bones represent the people of Israel. They are saying, 'We have become old, dry bones - all hope is gone.' Now give them this message from the Sovereign Lord: O my people, I will open your graves of exile and cause you to rise again. Then I will bring you back to the land of Israel. When this happens, O my people, you will know that I am the Lord."

Jerusalem is a Burden to the World

In Zechariah 12: 2-3 it says, "I will make Jerusalem and Judah like an intoxicating drink to all the nearby nations that send their armies to besiege Jerusalem. On that day I will make Jerusalem a heavy stone, a burden for the world. None of the nations who try to lift it will escape unscathed."

The Dramatic Increase in Travel and Knowledge

In a vision, God reveals to Daniel that in "the time of the end," travel and knowledge will increase: "But you, Daniel, keep this prophecy a secret; seal up the book until the time of the end. Many will rush here and there, and knowledge will increase" (Daniel 12: 4)

Exponential Growth Marks the Times

If a marked increase in travel and knowledge constitutes one of the most clearly observable signs of the end times, then the two are merely components of a much larger Sign of the end times - Exponential Growth.

Rise of the Gog / Magog Alliance

271

The prophet Ezekiel says, "This is another message that came to me from the Lord: 'Son of man, prophesy against Gog of the land of Magog, the prince who rules over the nations of Meshech and Tubal. Give him this message from the Sovereign Lord: Gog, I am your enemy! I will turn you around and put hooks into your jaws to lead you out to your destruction. I will mobilize your troops and cavalry and make you a vast and mighty horde, all fully armed. Persia, Ethiopia, and Libya will join you, too, with all their weapons. Gomer and all its hordes will also join you, along with the armies of Beth-togarmah from the distant north and many others' "(Ezekiel 38: 1-6). Who are these entities today? They are defined as: Magog, Meshech, and Tubal = Russia; Persia = Iran; Cush = Ethiopia; Put = Libya; Gomer = Turkey; and Beth-togarmah = Turkey, Armenia, and the Turkish-speaking people of Asia Minor.

The Rise of Global Government

According to the Book of Revelation, globalization involves more than just multinational corporations and global commerce. One day, a single man will rule all the people and nations on the earth: "And he was given authority to rule over every tribe and people and language and nation" (Revelation 13: 7).

<u>The Good News Preached Throughout the World</u>

Jesus spoke prophetically when He said these words, "And the Good News about the Kingdom will be preached throughout the whole world, so that all nations will hear it; and then the end will come" (Matthew 24: 14).

A Catholic Sign

Here I want to mention "The Sign of the Cross." This Sign is made by Catholics when they begin and end prayer. We also use it to bless ourselves before meals, and when we or others are entering perilous situations or requesting protection from harm. The Sign of the Cross identifies us as one, catholic (that is, universal) community of believers. It is an act of faith, demonstrating to all people our fidelity to the Holy Trinity, who is the Father, the Son, and the Holy Spirit.

Personal Signs

I will end this essay by showing how heavenly Signs may work in a person's life. Looking at my own experience, when I receive a Sign, it is usually because I need direction, or I am feeling anxious. It is then that I may ask the Lord for a specific Sign that affirms His loving presence in my life. In most cases, I want to be sure certain important decisions are correct according to His plan for me. Sometimes I'll ask a question, and if the Sign I requested appears, it tells me that the answer is yes, go ahead. If I don't receive a response, I continue in prayer, and I wait a day or two. Then, if no Sign appears, I might ask the question again but in a different manner. During such times, I may have to "wait on the Lord" for an answer, as advised in Psalm 130. But despite the wait, the Lord always reveals the direction that is best for me. Through Signs, He gives me confidence when I lack the courage to move forward, or when I feel uncertain about a choice I have made.

Sometimes a person may recognize a heavenly Sign, although he or she has not asked for one. Whenever this happens to me, I try to understand what the Lord is directing me to do. Case in point: if I am taking life too seriously and

274

getting too overwhelmed with the cares and responsibilities of this world, I may not be consciously aware of it. This is when I may get a series of out-of-the-ordinary Signs which occur in rapid succession. By their very exceptionality, they demand my attention, and it is only then I recognize these Signs as God-given. One thing that happens to me is that I suddenly start losing or misplacing things. I am sure this is a common experience for many, but since this is very unusual for me, I take special note of it whenever it happens. Only in doing so do I realize that, for my mental and physical wellbeing, it is time to slow down, to reevaluate how I use my time, and what thoughts I have allowed to enter my consciousness. Once I understand the problem and adjust my lifestyle accordingly, lost or misplaced items are no longer an issue.

In contrast to this, an exceptional event may occur only once, and the rarity of it alerts me to the presence of a heavenly Sign. It can be as simple as a sunlit, white egret flying solo overhead, the presence of a Monarch butterfly resting peacefully on my shoulder, or a brilliant rainbow suddenly appearing in the sky. It can be as exceptional as the formation of a heart-shaped cloud, finding a gold coin or even a four-leaf clover! A Sign can be the appearance of a certain flower with an amazing, intoxicating fragrance, or the abrupt arrival of a colorful songbird who announces his presence with an exquisite tune, then flies away. Although these are usually rare, one-time events, it is also possible that the same unlikely thing may reoccur over the course of days, weeks, or even longer. The effect this has on any observer is visceral and immediate, reinforcing just how outstanding and potent the Sign is against the backdrop of normal activity. As for me, I stay alert. That is when I realize the events manifesting as genuine Signs are pointing directly to the issue at hand. They never fail to remind me to remain serene and centered in God as He gently leads me forward.

Before my husband died, we had a particular affinity for gazing up at the night sky, observing the full moon. After his death, I moved to a new location and nowadays, when the full moon sets in the west, it magically appears in exact alignment with my bedroom window, as if the window had been placed there as the perfect frame for a glorious masterpiece! This has become a recurring ritual in my life, happening a few consecutive days every lunar month. Sometimes it occurs at three or four o'clock in the morning.

At such times, I suddenly wake up in bed just in time to view its full magnificence, without even having to move a muscle. The moon is so alive and bright, its brilliant rays flooding into my bedroom. And it feels as if my loved one has just "dropped by to say hello." Yes, it seems like my husband is truly present, and I am deeply touched by this amazing, reoccurring Sign.

Another unmistakable Sign comes from the Bible itself. And ironically, I just received a personal Sign about this as confirmation that what I am about to write is really true. Let me tell you about it. Currently, I am reading, "My Life with the Saints," by Fr. James Martin. Just as I started a new chapter, unbeknownst to me, I had arrived at the place in the book which speaks about this very topic! It is a topic I had decided to write about, but I hesitated, uncertain about how to begin. In the chapter now before me, the author indicated the precise approach to take. In addition, this reassuring Sign confirmed that no less than saints have used this technique to guide them. "Even Augustine relied on the method," we are told, and of course, he did so "to receive some divine guidance." Paraphrasing St. Augustine's thoughts from his classic work, "Confessions," Fr. James Martin concludes,

"For all his love of reason and philosophy," Augustine made use of the practice "of opening a book to a random page." This simple remedy is quite effective, and I will now explain how to do it.

First of all, it is wise to dispose oneself to receive the guidance sought. That means just sit quietly, centering yourself in a comfortable spot. This practice is sometimes called recollection. Then, humbly ask the Lord for help with your difficulty. After that, open to any random page in the Bible (no cheating allowed). The first passage your eyes fall upon is the one to read. It is uncanny how adroit these words are, seeming to offer direct guidance for the very issue at hand! Yet sometimes the application of random verses may not seem to fit. If you are stumped by what you read, try again, asking for clarity. The practice of receiving guidance from a book, most often the Bible or other sacred text, is indeed a practical one, since any inspired writing can and does provide unmistakable Signposts along the way.

Use Wisely

The use of Signs for guidance is only beneficial if used sparingly. This is because many things are resolved by themselves or by personal effort, requiring our "freewill" choice (see Lesson 1, "The Evolution of Freewill"). Heavy reliance on Signs can develop into a crutch or a habit, becoming an impediment to spiritual growth. So I would say, don't get carried away with it. There is certainly no need to "worry the Lord" over trivial or inconsequential matters.

All true Signs are messages from above. They are meant to give us more information about what is happening in our lives at a particular time. Or they may reveal something about a situation we anticipate happening in the near future. Just as often, they can point to something entirely new and unexpected, an idea we haven't thought about or imagined before. It is our job to pay close attention, to properly heed the message we get and to reflect on how it applies to our lives. This is what heavenly Signs are meant for.

LESSON SEVENTEEN

END-TIMES

PROPHECY

END-TIMES PROPHECY

" I am a fellow servant with you and with your brothers and sisters who hold to the testimony of Jesus. Worship God! For it is the Spirit of Prophecy who bears testimony to Jesus."

(Revelation 19: 10)

The Spirit of Prophecy

Truly, the Spirit of Prophecy "who bears testimony to Jesus," is alive and well today. As explained in Lesson 14, "Come Holy Spirit," prophetic messages given by the Spirit reveal mysteries. Their truth is collaborated by ancient writings from diverse sources which are centuries, even millennia old. Their forecasts come from modern-day witnesses who receive private revelations. Surprisingly, prophetic words are often spoken by ordinary people and young children. In this essay, I will look at a small number of the countless revelations and prophetic visions, both old and new, that exist today. This will be a general overview of various prophecies, not a detailed description of what the future may hold.

Nostradamus

Since the world has heard much about this famous seer, he needs no preamble, and there is no reason for me to recount his life story here. Suffice it to say that unfortunately, the Catholic Church during the time of Nostradamus, tried to persecute him. Although his father was a Catholic convert, the ignorance of the day did not allow for such a person as Nostradamus to prophesize about future events. Therefore, his prophecies were written in cryptic messages put together in vague quatrains. According to Wikipedia, "He devised a method of obscuring his meaning by using 'Virgilianised' syntax, word games, and a mixture of other languages such as Greek, Italian, and Latin." This was done in order to keep the local authorities from deeming him insane or accusing him of witchcraft. It is said that Nostradamus foretold the coming of both World Wars, the arrival of the airplane, and the demise of the twin towers in New York City. Nostradamus saw more cataclysmic events yet to come, many of which are expected to occur in our lifetime. He predicted a third and final Antichrist. Lastly, at some point in the not-too-distant future, he says that earth will

282

experience a bombardment of asteroids, which many scholars interpret as the end of the world. To find out more about Nostradamus and his extensive prophecies, I suggest the book, "The Complete Works of Nostradamus," by Michel de Nostredam himself. The collection contains nearly 400 pages of his prophetic quatrains.

The Great Pyramid of Egypt

A researcher named John Van Auken has studied the Great Pyramid for many years. In 2012, he wrote a book called, "2038: The Great Pyramid Timeline Prophecy." In it, Van Auken contends that in its innermost chamber, the Great Pyramid contains a timeline which began "when the morning stars sang together and all the sons of God shouted for joy" (Job: 38: 7). The timeline culminates when humanity evolves from "Human Being to Star-God." After studying the precise years on this timeline, the author concludes that 2038 marks the end of the Great Pyramid's timeline prophecy for humanity. Basically, this means that 2038 is "the end of the age." Van Auken describes what follows as "an age of enlightenment." As strange as this prophecy sounds, it has its parallel in both ancient and modern Christian prophecies, which we shall soon discover.

Ordinary People

God grants to some the unexpected gift of prophecy. As stated earlier, this gift may be given to mere children or to ordinary, non-religious adults, as well as mystics and saints. In his book, "Christian Prophecy: The Post Biblical Tradition" (2007), author Niels Hvidt looks at normal, everyday people, both past and present, who have received divine revelations. He presents a twenty-first century case study, that of Vassula Ryden. She says she rarely thought of God before she was converted instantly on November 28, 1985, when she experienced a tingling in her right hand and an invisible presence. She proceeded to write down what she experienced at that moment, and she heard the words, "I am your guardian angel; my name is Daniel." From this one experience came years of visions and revelations. Vassula has had no theological training, and this is seen by the author as an advantage: "Because she did not have any merits or assets...all initiative thereby would be Christ's." Today, Vassula believes her mission is to unite the Churches of East and West, Orthodox and Roman Catholic traditions. Her case has been studied extensively, but of course; she has detractors. Both Eastern and Western branches of the Church advise extreme prudence in the matter, since currently, neither side is willing to accept Vassula as a true prophet.

Contrary to the above circumstance, it is universally accepted and recognized that a spiritual encounter with Mother Mary occurred in 1917 at Fatima, Portugal, to three unschooled children. This particular apparition has been well examined for its authenticity, and today the site is an international destination for pilgrims. More recently, Our Lady appeared to children at Garabandal, a remote village in northern Spain in 1961. Then she appeared in 1981 at Medjugorje, a town in southwestern Bosnia -Herzegovina, about 12 miles east of the border with Croatia. All three of these remarkable visitations are said to announce significant prophetic decrees. Although the Church has not yet taken a position as to whether the two most recent apparitions are indeed supernatural in origin, it has long since given official approval for the Fatima events, deeming them authentic visions. What I wish to note here is that in all three cases, the messages are basically the same, yet exceedingly simple: believe in God, turn away from evil, and live good lives. If humanity does not do this, there will be dire times ahead. In the Fatima prophecies, Mary provides reason for hope: "In the end Russia will be converted and my Immaculate Heart with triumph."

During the same timeframe, the Blessed Virgin Mary appeared to poor, illiterate children in other locales as well. She came to eight young visionaries at Kibeho, Rwanda, Africa, begging for change and warning that a horrendous event would occur there if her admonitions were not heeded. This tragedy happened thirteen years later in 1994, when Rwanda experienced a mass genocide. Another apparition occurred there in 1982. This time Jesus Himself appeared to a young African, pagan boy named Segatashya, who was given a mission "to remind mankind how to reach Heaven." After following Jesus' instructions, Segatashya was murdered during the Rwandan genocide. Two excellent books about "Our Lady of Kibeho" (2008) and "The Boy Who Met Jesus" (2011) were written by Immaculee Ilibagiza, herself a survivor of the genocide which took the lives of almost all her family members.

Returning to the Garabandal and Medjugorje events, the visionaries, now adults, tell us that an "Illumination of Conscience"is coming soon to the world. According to them, this will be an experience everyone will feel in their deepest soul. It will show us the condition of our lives in the same way that God sees us. It is meant to help us correct whatever problems or vices we have yet to overcome. Although no exact dates are given, signs of the nearness of this event are evident today. What coincides with the "Illumination" is a "Warning," and what follows it is a great "Miracle." The "Miracle" will be a permanent, supernatural sign which can be photographed, but it cannot be scientifically explained. The whole world will witness these extraordinary events. Since they come from above, no one will be able to disprove their heavenly origin. However, conspiracy theorists and other skeptics will deny the "Miracle," insisting it is a hologram or some other technological trick. Despite their witnessing the unequivocal truth, nay-sayers will continue to spout lies.

About What's Coming

Christine Watkins wrote a book in 2019 about the "Warning" and the "Illumination of Conscience," giving her impression of how these concurrent events will unfold ("The Warning: Testimonies and Prophecies of The Illumination of Conscience"). First of all, she tells us that less than a year before the predicted "Miracle," there will be smaller, but no less miraculous signs in the sky heralding the coming events. Much earlier prophecies also forecast the appearance of "holy signs in the heavens" (see the words of Mathias Lang below). When these signs reach their peak, the "Warning" and the "Illumination of Conscience" will descend upon the earth. They will be such earth-shattering events that millions of people will be instantly converted. Although this phenomenon is rooted in both traditional and contemporary Catholic prophecy, I recently learned that Protestants too, have received a similar revelation, one that closely resembles the "Illumination of Conscience" foreseen at Garabandal and Medjugorje. In what they call the "Golden Global Glory," these modern-day, visionary Christians expect a mighty outpouring of the Holy Spirit upon all humanity to occur at any moment. If these things come to pass as predicted, Churches everywhere will be overflowing with people wanting to find out what happened to them, and what it portends for their souls. As you can imagine, all Christian believers who are aware of these impending events, anticipate them with great excitement. It is said the experience will be equivalent to a "Second Pentecost." (See Lesson 14, "Come Holy Spirit").

Immediately following these amazing events, the world will enjoy a period of peace. Its duration depends on how many will embrace the enormous import of what they have witnessed, and for how long they will be willing to adopt the new code of conduct which they clearly saw was needed in their lives. We are told to look at this period of peace as a "Time of Mercy." Unfortunately, if the prophecies hold true, it will be short-lived. Here the visionaries from Garabandal report they were given another warning: After the "Miracle" takes place, if people still refuse to alter their behavior significantly with no fundamental change, they will bring upon themselves a horrific "Chastisement." The visionaries call this next phase a "Time of Justice." Again, these predictions conform to prophecies of a much earlier period. I have briefly described some of them below under the heading, "Prophecies of the Saints."

It is noteworthy that the timeframe for these revelations to take place dovetails nicely with the Great Pyramid prophecy timeline about which John Van Auken wrote. Moreover, there is another author whose timeline also agrees. This author makes a connection between the coming Warning and the date 2038, although there is no evidence that he is aware of Van Auken's research. Bruce Cyr's book is called, "After the Warning to 2038" (2017). In it, he looks almost exclusively at the copious ancient prophecies of the saints. The author sifts through their messages, and aligns them with biblical prophecies, thus deriving his own suggested timeline. I find it fascinating that both Mr. Van Auken and Mr. Cyr independently decided upon the same conclusive year: 2038. But just yesterday, as I was watching the Travel Channel on TV, I learned that Nostradamus too, had pronounced the same year, 2038, as apocalyptic. Since he wrote in symbols, the date is clad in astrological language, with "Mercury, Jupiter, and Mars in fire (signs)." Thus, according to experts who study Nostradamus' prophecies, he pinpointed an exact date: June 20, 2038.

Prophecies of the Saints

As I have suggested, there are many commentaries in and out of print which represent an incredible dossier of factual documents, compiled hundreds of years ago, that seem to suddenly come to life, and that point to the events of our modern age. In fact, it is amazing that so many of these prophecies can only find relevance in the present day, and at no other time in history, as we shall see.

290

To begin the discussion, I deliberately chose obscure, unknown prophetic voices to underscore the immediacy of their words for our times. The first is Mathias Lang, also known in some accounts as Stormberger. He was illiterate with no education and lived in Bavaria between 1735 and 1820. Among other things, his writings predict World War I, and also the new modes of transportation that would develop during that era. Lang declares, "When the iron road passing through the forest is built, and the iron hound passes the deserted bay, afterwards, when the wagon without horse and shaft travels, and people fly like birds in the sky, and when the silver fish flies over our forest…then is the war year." My source for this quote and the ones that follow is, "Catholic Prophecies for the End Times: Part One," compiled in 2005 by Sean Patrick Bloomfield. The editor notes, "The iron road" and "iron hound" are probably the railroads and trains. The "wagon without horse or shaft" is the automobile, and "people flying like birds" predicts the airplane. The "silver fish" is probably the German Zeppelin which became popular at the beginning of World War I."

Mathias Lang writes: "After the great War, there will be no peace." Then he continues to make accurate predictions about the second World War. Looking further into the future, Lang remarks, "When women walk around in pants and men have become effeminate, so that one will no longer be able to tell men from women, then the time is near." The time for what? Here he says, "there will be holy signs in the heavens..." Could this be the signal for the "Warning" and the "Illumination" to come? Regrettably, Lang's statements indicate that, even after witnessing marvelous "holy signs," mankind will not change much. Looking ahead, he foresees a devastating third World War which will be "the end of many nations." Lang's descriptions seem to mirror what is expounded in the biblical Book of Revelation, adding some thorny details. Moreover, his testimonies specifically mention the Old Testament prophet Daniel, warning that this is the period in history when Daniel's prophecies are fulfilled. What Lang goes on to portray sounds very much like the coming "Chastisement" spoken about by the Garabandal seers. Even though Lang's short-term predictions are about devastation and ruin, he announces that afterwards, "A good time will come," that which is "Loved by Jesus Christ, and holy men will do wonders." He goes on to say, "Once people have their faith again, a long period of peace will follow. Those who are still alive will be given housing and as much land as they need."

Mitar Tarabich was a Serbian peasant who lived from 1829 to 1899. His predictions announced the Serbian conflicts starting before World War I, and those continuing up to the present day, including the establishment of Croatia and Bosnia-Hercegovina. He says during the End-Times, "People will drive in rigs to the Moon and stars. They will look for life, but life similar to ours they will not find. It will be there, but they will not be able to understand and see that it is life." He condemns the future age by saying, "Souls will not be possessed by the devil, but by something much worse. They will believe that their delusion is real truth, although there will be no truth in their heads." (See Lesson 9, "Finding Truth"). The prophet's harsh words continue, "Only weaklings will be born, and nobody will be strong enough to give birth to a real hero." He goes on to exclaim, "Everyone will say, 'I know, I know, because I am learned and smart,' but nobody will know anything," and "Those who will learn to read and write different books with numbers will think that they know the most. These learned men will let their lives be led by their calculations, and they will do and live exactly how these numbers tell them." To me, this describes today's global economies, where everything is tied to charts and algorithms, especially as they relate to the stock market and social media. Furthermore, "The more people know, the less and less they will love and care for each other. Hatred will be so great between them that they will care more for their different gadgets than for their relatives. Man will trust his gadget more than his neighbor." Electronic devices are, of course, the "gadgets" we totally rely on today, so this statement really hits home! Finally, the prophet concludes there will be terrible years of pestilence and war, but after that, "only one country at the end of the world, surrounded by a great sea, as big as our Europe, will live in peace, without any troubles...Upon it or over it, not a single ball will explode." We are left to wonder, is this country the United States or Australia?

Finally, I will briefly highlight Abbot Joachim Merlin, who lived around 1530, John of the Cleft Rock, a 14th century prophet, St. Nilus, who lived around 400 AD, and lastly, Blessed Anna Maria Taigi, who prophesized in the mid-1800's. Each makes predictions about the future of the Church and especially the Popes who will reign during the

End-Times. The Abbot also speaks about the coming of the much-anticipated reunification of the Eastern Orthodox and Western churches, which, as I mentioned earlier, is visionary Vassula Ryden's avowed mission. Like Mathias Lang, the Abbot forecasts that in the end, nations will flourish: "The true God of the Jews, our Lord Jesus Christ, will make everything prosper beyond all human hope, because God alone can and will pour down on the wounds of humanity the oily balm of sweetness." This prediction offers a wonderful conclusion to an incredibly dark and dreadful period, an optimistic finale shared by other seers as well.

So, as I just explained, we are told that before lasting peace can occur, there will be much trouble ahead. John of the Cleft Rock describes this period, one that looks very similar to our present day. This is when "the Pope with his cardinals will have to flee Rome in tragic circumstances. The Pope will die a cruel death in his exile." Some of us recognize this statement as synonymous with the "Third Secret of Fatima." Moving on to St. Nilus, we get more information about this time period. His prophecy declares, "The advent of the Antichrist approaches, and people's minds will grow cloudy from carnal passions, and dishonor and lawlessness will grow stronger... Lust, homosexuality, secret deeds, and murder will rule society." He laments, "At that future time, due to the power of such great crimes and licentiousness, people will be deprived of the Holy Spirit, which they received in Holy Baptism and equally of remorse" (see Lesson 14, "Come Holy Spirit"). St. Nilus tells us people "will spend their lives in comfort without knowing, poor souls, that it is the deceit of the Antichrist. And, the impious one! He will so complete science with vanity that it will go off the right path and lead people to lose faith in the existence of God." That is certainly our state of affairs today!

Continuing with the prophecies of St. Nilus, he records a vision of what I think is already happening: "The all-good God will see the downfall of the human race and *will shorten days* for the sake of those few who are being saved, because the enemy wants to lead the chosen into temptation, if that is possible..." Does "shortening the days" mean that time actually speeds up? Here I recall a prediction in John Van Auken's book, based on the Great Pyramid timeline. The author briefly mentions that time will move faster in the last days, saying, "Time speeds up – the same amount of activities happen in one-twelfth of the time they used to take." This shortening of time is echoed by the biblical prediction found in Matthew 24: 22. It also harkens back to warnings given at Garabandal, and to the prophetic words written in the Book of Revelation. Finally, St. Nilus tells us that after these terrible times, "then the sword of chastisement will suddenly appear and kill the perverter and his servants." Perhaps this is further evidence of a future time of true and lasting peace.

It is generally accepted that what is called the "Chastisement" will be accompanied by a period known as the "Three Days of Darkness." Blessed Anna Maria Taigi, a relatively well-known seer in prophetic circles, expounds on these terrifying days: "God will send two punishments: one will be in the form of wars, revolutions and other evils; it shall originate on earth. The other will be sent from Heaven. There shall come over the whole earth an intense darkness lasting three days and three nights." To me, these three days and nights of complete darkness signify the sign of Jonah, which in turn, mirror Jesus's three days in the tomb (see the previous Lesson, "Heavenly Signs"). In her writings, Anne Maria Taigi has much more to say about the coming "Three Days of Darkness," but the important thing to remember is this: Those who are pure of heart will light blessed candles during this fearful time and, by praying to God for mercy, they will survive the horrific ordeal. But only blessed candles in the hands of the righteous will light. All others who don't avail themselves of this sacred remedy will perish. Again, we are told that afterwards, there will be universal peace.

Ancient Biblical Prophecy

There is an entire field of prophecy originating from Jewish sources, which predict events from the beginning of record keeping until the end of time. The first great prophets were, of course, the Hebrew prophets like Abraham, Moses, Isaiah, Ezekiel, and Daniel. Upon their rich legacy, the Christian Bible was built. Since we already know these ancient texts foretold significant events, we naturally assume they predicted the arrival of the Jewish Messiah. And so they did. As explained in Lesson 16, "Heavenly Signs," Jesus' coming was announced in many Jewish writings well before the time came. Today, some of these writings comprise the Old Testament of the present-day Bible. Among the most notable passages describing Jesus are the ones found in Isaiah 53 and Psalm 22. According to Sid Roth, the Christian convert from Judaism whom I spoke about in other essays,

298

"There are over three hundred predictions of the coming of the suffering servant Messiah" contained in the ancient Hebrew texts. ("They Thought for Themselves: Ten Amazing Jews," 2009).

As a benefit from studying the New Testament Gospels, we are able to see the early Jewish prophecies in a new light. We can connect the dots from the ancient Israelites (Old Covenant) to the coming of Christ (New Covenant). Here's just one example: After Jesus rose from the dead, He appeared to two disciples who were traveling to Emmaus. They did not recognize Him yet, but He proceeded to instruct them as they walked along the road. Finally, Jesus exclaimed to them, 'How foolish you are, and how slow to believe all that the prophets have spoken! Did not the Messiah have to suffer these things and then enter his glory?' And beginning with Moses and all the prophets, He explained to them what was said in all the Scriptures concerning Himself." This passage is from Luke 24: 25-27.

Ever since that time, Jewish people insist they do not accept Jesus as the true Messiah, the very One who was foretold by their own prophets. However, not all accent to this belief. More and more of today's Jewish people are well-read and open-minded about this. Many of them have actually concluded that Jesus was indeed the true Messiah whom they were waiting for. These Jews refer to themselves as "Messianic Jews," or "Jews for Jesus." I suggest reading Sid Roth's books and going to his website for a complete understanding of this hopeful trend.

Biblical prophecy has more to say about events that are still to come. After Jesus ascended into Heaven, His teachings about the End-Times were recorded in several New Testament gospels. Matthew 24, for example, gives both warnings and predictions about the future, while in Matthew 25: 1-13, Jesus presents a parable to illustrate our need for readiness as the time draws near. He tells the story of the virgins who were awaiting the Bridegroom's arrival. Ten virgins were foolish and ten were wise. The wise ones carried ample oil for their lamps, but the foolish ones did not. We are told the Bridegroom was long delayed in coming, and while the virgins waited and slept, their lamps went out. The wise virgins had brought along extra oil for their lamps, but the others ran out. When the Bridegroom showed up unexpectedly, the ten foolish virgins had no time to buy more oil, and being unprepared, they were left behind. On the other hand, the wise virgins who had come prepared with sufficient oil for their lamps, were invited in. (see Lesson 7, "Practice Vigilance").

Regarding the Book of Revelation, it is recognized as a collection of prophetic visions which Christians believe will occur at the End-Times. The book was written by St. John the Divine during his exile on the island of Patmos. Although some say Revelation is a purely literal description of future events, others believe it is purely symbolic, and should not be taken literally at all. It is true that Revelation speaks in obscure and symbolic language, but nevertheless, it clearly foretells the coming of the Antichrist, two Witnesses, and the second coming of Christ. Yet the chapters are probably not in chronological order and are veiled in mysticism, so they are difficult to decipher. Different authorities interpret the Book in a number of ways, and to my knowledge, there is no definitive sequential order of events that has been firmly established. What is very certain is that a battle is raging between good and evil, and it will reach its peak "at the end of the age." Thankfully, God's truth and justice will ultimately prevail. For more on this, see Lesson 2, "The Triumph of Justice."

The Seven Jewish Feasts

The Seven Feasts which the Jewish people celebrate annually are: Passover, Unleavened Bread, First Fruits, Pentecost, Trumpets, Day of Atonement, and Tabernacles. Many online sources identify a correspondence between these seven traditional feasts, with the end of Jesus' life and the prophecies written in the Book of Revelation. A website called "Rapture Forums" explains: "The first three Feasts represent the death, burial, and resurrection of the Lord. The order of feasts is laid out in specific order by God to simulate what will take place. The final feasts are connected with the Holy Spirit, followed by a Tribulation period, the Coming of the Lord, and His reign on earth." The commentary that follows below is taken directly from the "Rapture Forums" website:

> 1)   Starting with <u>Passover</u>, (Pesach) this represents the crucifixion of Jesus. In Egypt, it represented the sacrifice of the spotless lamb, so the Angel of Death would pass over the homes that had the blood displayed as instructed. Today, Jesus is our Spotless Lamb that was sacrificed.

2) <u>Unleavened Bread,</u> (Hag Hamtzah) represents the burial of Christ. In Egypt, bread was to be made without leavening in preparation for leaving Egypt rapidly when the time came.

3) <u>First Fruits,</u> (Bikkurim) is resurrection from the grave. In Leviticus, it was to represent the First Portion of the harvest. Jesus is our First Fruit as He was first to rise in our new Covenant which by the way, does not replace the Abrahamic covenant.

4) <u>Pentecost</u> or Feast of Weeks, (Saavuot) is the arrival of the Holy Spirit 50 days after the resurrection. The original was when God met with Moses on Mt. Sinai.

5) <u>Trumpets,</u> (Rosh Hashanah /Yom Teruah) announcements to be made. In Numbers 10:2, God told Moses to have two trumpets of silver from a single hammered piece made for assembly and directing travel. Today, we await this trumpet to signal the Rapture (1 Thessalonians 4). It will be very rapid, and I believe only heard

by those who have accepted Jesus. Some believe this may be so far off, but whatever it is it will be calling us to Jesus in the clouds. Note: this is NOT any trumpet in the 7 Trumpet Judgments of Revelation. This is the last trumpet as given in 1 Corinthians 15.

6)   Atonement, (Yom Kippur) represents the Second Coming of Christ where He actually sets foot on the earth. In the Rapture, believers rise up to meet Him in the Clouds. In Moses' day, sacrifice was made to atone for the people's sins. This also signifies Satan being defeated at the end of the Tribulation.

7)   Tabernacles, (Sukkot) represents Jesus' 1000-year reign on earth. In Moses time, temporary shelters were set up as a celebration of their leaving Egypt, and they were to be lived in for 7 days each year. In the future, all earth's inhabitants will go to Jerusalem to worship the Lord annually. (Zechariah 14: 16)

"Rapture Forums" ends its assessment by saying, "Even

though Christians do not celebrate the Jewish Holiday Feasts, they are very significant as you can see. It's good to know what their original meanings were and now as to how they pertain to believers."

The webpage continues, "We are at the threshold of the Trumpet that is about to sound. Just looking at Bible prophecy and comparing it to what's happening today is our greatest sign of this event's rapid approach. The alignment of the Ezekiel 38 coalition is in place for the first time in history. Lawlessness, people turning away from the Lord, increased earthquake and volcano activity, wars and rumors of war and changes in the weather pattern are evidence, just to name a few."

Prophecy for Today

The various apocalyptic views I have presented in this essay on prophecy are food for thought. Because they have been researched and shared by many scholars and experts in the field, it is worth taking these writings seriously. Although they are subject to different interpretations from time to time, they contain an underlying unity and an internal consistency.

Prophecy is an area of study that is under constant

scrutiny; this can be both good and bad: Good because authentic research provides significant new facts; bad because there are always people whose sole purpose is to debunk or misinterpret what they do not understand. These biased sources tend to misrepresent, distort, and mislead, while others proclaim that only science is the ultimate source of truth. In our relentless search for meaning, we must always be vigilant against such protagonists, lest we allow science, or anything else, to become our god. (See Lesson 5, "Choose Life"). In the end, the realities that have been revealed by authentic prophecy cannot be suppressed, and the more people who are aware of their significance and timeliness, the better this world will be.

Alda St. James, Author

Alda St. James

ABOUT THE AUTHOR

Alda St. James is an artist, poet, counselor, master goldsmith, and author. Her first publication is a book of poetry called, *"Listen to Love: Reflective Poems for All Seasons."* She holds a Fine Arts degree from Syracuse University and a master's degree in Education and Counseling from the University of Idaho. It has always been her desire to champion the causes of art, beauty, and harmony in everyday life. She does this through many forms of artistic expression, following her intuitive and creative inclinations wherever they lead. Her Italian name, Alda, means "richly blessed." In order to bring more joy and love into the world, Alda and her husband Jim, appreciated the opportunity of becoming foster and adoptive parents. During the years they spent working with abused and neglected children and teens, this effort eventually became their primary mission.

The recent passing of her husband left a void in Alda's life. But the loss invited a refreshing return to writing, both lyrical poetry and the reflective essays found in this book. Her delightful illustrations are found in another publication, a *"Birthstone Coloring Book"* designed especially for children. Being an incurable optimist, the author continues to fill the void with an incredible burst of creative energy, producing artistic works which welcome a promising season of renewal and hope.

You can learn more about Alda St. James at her website here: aldastjames.com

Made in the USA
Las Vegas, NV
17 December 2021